Praise for *Saints of Feather and Fang: How the Animals We Love and Fear Connect Us to God*

"Caryn Rivadeneira finds holiness in wild and domesticated creatures. There are cuddly pets here, but there are coyotes, hedgehogs, and snakes as well. This is an honest God-experience. We feel stroked or companioned at times, but frightened and mystified just as often."

—Jon M. Sweeney, author of *Feed the Wolf*
and *The Complete Francis of Assisi*

"For curious animal lovers who cherish God, talented author Caryn Rivadeneira has compiled a beautifully inspiring look at how creatures of the animal kingdom serve as spiritual guides for the growth of human souls. Surprising and original, it is a glorious reflection on humanity's connection to the joy and power of the Lord's 'feather and fang' fellowship."

—Patricia Raybon, award-winning author of
*My First White Friend: Confessions on Race,
Love, and Forgiveness* and *I Told the Mountain
to Move: Learning to Pray So Things Change*

"From comparing God's love to that of a 'mama eagle,' to likening pit bulls to the good Samaritan and exploring the 'anywhen' of liminal places, *Saints of Feather and Fang* is full of surprises. Author, animal lover, and seminarian Caryn Rivadeneira is fierce, funny, and fresh in these pages as she examines what animals can teach us about our Creator."

—Jennifer Grant, author of
Dimming the Day and other books

"Animals have always been my teachers, my mentors, my inspiration. In them, I see the face of the Creator. Caryn Rivadeneira's sometimes sweet, sometimes funny, always touching stories remind us that each of God's creatures is sacred and holy, with lessons to teach us all about God's love."
—Sy Montgomery, author of *The Soul of an Octopus* and *How to Be a Good Creature*

"The psalmist tells us that the heavens declare the glory of God, but what does that really mean? From pit bulls and snakes to hedgehogs and sheepdogs, this book will inspire the reader to imagine and explore what creation might be proclaiming about God."
—April Fiet, author of *The Sacred Pulse: Holy Rhythms for Overwhelmed Souls*

"Caryn Rivadeneira's sparkling mosaic of stories, science, and Scripture about animals will have you seeing God in the octopi, donkeys, and crows. Warmly, and with wit, she reveals One Great Love streaming through everything that breathes, redeeming us all, together."
—Gayle Boss, author of *All Creation Waits: The Advent Mystery of New Beginnings* and *Wild Hope: Stories for Lent from the Vanishing*

"Caryn Rivadeneira writes that animals help us to understand and see God's greatness and goodness better; this book did just that for me. *Saints of Feather and Fang* is a book to be savored."
—Suzy Flory, *New York Times* bestselling author or coauthor of sixteen books

SAINTS OF FEATHER
AND FANG

SAINTS

OF

FEATHER

AND

FANG

*HOW the ANIMALS WE LOVE and FEAR
CONNECT US to GOD*

CARYN
RIVADENEIRA

Broadleaf Books

Minneapolis

To Henrik, Greta, and Fredrik

Contents

CONTENTS

INTRODUCTION

All creatures of our God and King
Lift up your voice with us and sing.
— *Saint Francis of Assisi*

I have always loved animals. Family lore tells of me reaching for our giant husky-shepherd mix the moment I came home from the hospital, refusing to speak to grown-ups but happily running to greet every strange dog I encountered, and hiding from the costumed characters at Disney World, instead following tiny chipmunks into the bushes.

When my own memories kick in, the story doesn't change. I rejected baby dolls and Barbies, preferring the company of the piles of stuffed animals

1

that overwhelmed my bedroom. My most perused book was *National Geographic Book of Mammals.* I'd spread the volumes open and study the pictures and information, returning again and again to the spread on bats, hoping to squelch my fear. (It worked! More on this later.)

The stories demonstrating my deep love of animals are endless. A million spring to mind. But since this is a book about animals *and* God, it's important that I mention this: though I have been a Christian nearly my whole life, I have not always loved Jesus.

You heard that right.

I was baptized as an infant in a Lutheran congregation and taken to church most Sundays of my youth. I had a mystical experience with God at age seven that led me to believe in God's actual realness and presence. All this time, I would have *said* I loved Jesus. But I never really did. Here's how I know.

My grandmother died when I was seventeen. She was a devout Christian woman, although she didn't go to church. Not in the years I knew her, at least. TV preachers were her thing. I still have notebooks filled with notes and questions she'd jot down as she watched church from the comfort of her chair.

My grandma had some weird beliefs. In fact, I believe the best Christians do. But one that I never questioned was her stance that if dogs weren't in heaven, she didn't want to go there either.

This made complete and total sense to me—until, that is, my late twenties, when I mentioned this bit of theology to a Christian acquaintance. She laughed and then said, "Good thing we'll be so happy to see Jesus, we won't even care if our dogs aren't there!"

Total gut punch.

It was the worst thing I'd ever heard.

But that was when I realized I *didn't* love Jesus. I believed in Jesus (in a wrestling, antagonistic sort of way). I followed Jesus (in a middle-class American sort of way). And I proclaimed Jesus (in my reserved way).

But I didn't love him. Because I could not for one second fathom being happier to see Jesus than I would've been to see Sven or Faith or Gus.

It wasn't even close.

But it wasn't just the idea of not being happy to see my dogs that threw me. When I gave heaven or a new earth any thought, I never cared about mansions or streets of gold. Yes, I wanted reunions with loved ones and conversations with Cleopatra (I believe in a big God). For sure, I wanted relationships with no suffering.

But mostly, I wanted the lion lying down with the yearling. I wanted the child playing with the cobra. I wanted the garden of Eden where I could scratch the cheeks of a mama grizzly and nuzzle a moose.

That was heaven.

But still, I felt bad when I realized I didn't love Jesus as I thought I did or should have. So I did what any good Christian would have done: I took it to Jesus himself. I asked for forgiveness. I asked for help. I said, "If I don't love you as I should, help me."

Of course, there was no immediate change. No thunderbolt. No new heart.

But when, ten or so years later, I walked into the kitchen to find our one-hundred-pound Rottweiler dead on the kitchen floor, I dropped to the ground to touch Bob's huge snout, to confirm the lack of breath. I had often wondered if he would die with his beloved tennis ball in his mouth. He didn't. But in my despair, a sudden and overwhelming sense of calm came over me. An image flashed through my mind—a picture of Jesus throwing a tennis ball to our sweet dog in heaven.

And I loved Jesus for it.

———

God has always used weird things to shape my theology. Often, it's been through suffering. Other times, it's through the music of the Indigo Girls or some old-time hymn writer. Usually, though, God shapes and guides my thinking through my great loves: my husband, my children, and animals—both those that have lived in my house and those in the wide world beyond.

At least, when I'm paying attention.

I've written books about suffering. I've already overshared personal stories about my family (and my children are old enough now to be fully off-limits—although perhaps they should have always been). My thoughts about the Indigo Girls and hymn writers remain too unformed to write about yet. But being in the mood to explore more about how God uses weird things to reveal Godself, I'm inclined to let the animals do some talking, to explore and listen to the ways all creatures proclaim the glories and wonders of our Creator.

Of course, my desire is in good company. From the psalmists to Saint Francis to British veterinarian and author James Herriot, animal-loving humans have long appreciated and written about what animals "say" about God. When we pay attention, we see that animals can teach, show, and model aspects of our Creator we might otherwise miss. I have to believe this is the way God intended it.

After all, God may have made humans in God's image and given humans some kind of "dominion" over animals, but throughout Scripture, writers look to the animal kingdom for metaphors for God. (Of course, what this dominion was meant to look like is hotly contested. But no matter our interpretation, we've clearly messed up caring for the earth in more ways than we can count.) Jesus, who was the Lion of Judah and Lamb of God, made it clear that servants—suffering ones, even—make wonderful teachers. In the Bible, the promises of rescue, redemption, and rebirth apply to *all* creation. Not just us humans. And so, although only humans go to church and write creeds, though only we attend seminaries and get baptized, all creatures share the ability to recognize and praise our Creator. Psalm 148:7–14 offers a beautiful picture of this:

> *Praise the Lord from the earth,*
> *you sea monsters and all deeps,*
> *fire and hail, snow and frost,*
> *stormy wind fulfilling his command!*
> *Mountains and all hills,*
> *fruit trees and all cedars!*
> *Wild animals and all cattle,*
> *creeping things and flying birds!*
> *Kings of the earth and all peoples,*
> *princes and all rulers of the earth!*
> *Young men and women alike,*
> *old and young together!*

Let them praise the name of the Lord,
for his name alone is exalted;
his glory is above earth and heaven.

Sea monsters. Creeping things. Wild animals. Flying
birds. Amazing! All creatures can praise God and
thus know something about God's good heart.

We can learn these things if we pay attention.
When I finally started listening to what animals had
to say about things like love—what love looks and
feels like—I discovered I may have loved Jesus all
along.

Which is why and how this book came to be.
While many people view animal stories as mere "feel-
good" or "human interest" pieces that exist to warm
our hearts and cheer our days, the human experience
with the animals we love and fear runs much deeper.
I suspect we all understand this—and not just us pet
lovers. I mean, we go to zoos and aquariums; we
take trips into nature and get excited about spotting
wild creatures for good reason: animals are good for
our souls because they *move* our souls and reveal our
Creator.

That is why this book is titled—somewhat
cheekily—*Saints of Feather and Fang*. Of course, animals are not actual saints (well, with the exception of
Saint Guinefort, a snake-killing, child-saving French

chien whose grave was the site of many a miracle). But the saints do tell us something about God. And they point us to God. As someone who has loved and lived with animals my whole life, been involved with animal rescue, and written children's books about emotional support dogs who work miracles on the regular (*Helper Hounds*!) and adventurous penguins who teach about conservation (*Edward & Annie*!), I have seen that animals mirror the saints in many ways.

We're going to look at the ways animals teach us about love; about God's rescue plans; about vices and virtues; about delight, adaptability, and the importance of instinct; about fear, creativity, and abundance; about those liminal spaces between earth and heaven; and about redemption. To make this journey, we need to open our minds, our hearts, our senses. We might need to think differently about the typical ways we encounter God—or view animals. But animals are one of God's great gifts. All nature speaks and points to our Creator if we are willing to notice. We can learn so much about this life and our God if we pay some attention to these amazing saints of feather and fang.

1

LOVE

WHEN GOD STIRS THE NEST

After suffering a second stroke, my friend's mother was largely unable to communicate with her family. Words came out hard and slow if at all. Day after day, my friend Meg would sit next to her mother's hospital bed, reading her mother's favorite books and speaking words of love and comfort. Meg would ask questions, desperate to hear one word. To no avail.

That is, until one afternoon Meg's mother cried as she gasped out one word to her daughter. "Bill," she said. "Bill . . ."

"Bill?" Meg asked. "Mom, who is Bill?"

There was no answer, of course. But again and again, her mom moaned, "Bill . . ." as the tears flowed.

In her distress, Meg's mind raced to what could be causing her mother to cry like this. A long-lost love? Or a long-lost child? Was her mother trying to tell her about a baby she'd given up? Is that what Meg would learn?

She texted her dad and her siblings: "Mom is crying about a 'Bill.' Anyone have any clues?"

No one did.

Meg's mind continued to reel—until a nurse walked in. Meg's mom looked at the nurse and moaned, "Bill . . ."

"Oh don't worry," the nurse said. "Bill will be here again next week. Tuesday, I think."

Meg was stunned. In all her wonderings, never once had she imagined *Bill* had made his way to her mother's hospital room.

"Who's Bill?" Meg asked the nurse, nervous to hear the answer.

"Bill the therapy pony," the nurse said. "All the patients love him."

"I laughed for ten minutes straight," Meg told me later. Never once since her strokes had her mother *cried* about her children or grandchildren. She hadn't cried over visits from friends or siblings. Her mom didn't even really *like* animals, and yet Bill the therapy pony managed to elicit tears. "I couldn't believe it!" Meg said.

I could. In fact, the story didn't surprise me at all.

Of course Bill the therapy pony would cause that reaction. And not just because miniature horses (not really ponies) are ridiculously cute. In addition to helping people like Meg's mom recover motor and speech skills, therapy animals like Bill, through both training and instinct, offer essential human needs in times of suffering. Bill brought comfort, joy, and smiles. But ultimately, Bill brought *love*. Without judgment. Without worry lines. Without breaking down in sobs of grief. These things are all but impossible for concerned children, grandchildren, siblings, and friends to do for a loved one in that moment. Bill the therapy pony's face never betrayed him. His whinny never came out higher-pitched than intended. Bill could simply be calm, joyful, and present for Meg's mom during a troubling time.

In many ways, Bill was the loving presence of God. And who wouldn't cry about that?

———

Whether animals show or feel love has been a subject of debate for probably as long as humans have loved animals. Though certainly humans (and the earliest humans) first admired or even loved animals long before dogs became our friends, our earliest evidence of humanity's love for animals—outside of our bellies—goes back at least fifteen thousand years. While human appreciation and love for animals from afar (or as dinner) probably goes back millions of years, it was around 13,000 BCE that, researchers estimate, our nomadic ancestors wandered into wolf territory, and a few friendly wolves decided to wander into theirs—perhaps lured by the smell of sizzling meat or simply company. And according to writer Jeffrey Kluger, when we fell for these friendly wolves, we fell fast.

Kluger writes that though our ancestors didn't understand the genetics of what made certain wolves friendly (scientists are only touching the surface of this now), they did know that "every now and then, one or two of the midsize scavengers with the long muzzles that came nosing around their campfires would gaze at them with a certain attentiveness, a certain loving neediness, and that it was awfully hard to resist them. So they welcomed those few in from the cold and eventually came to call them dogs."

While the advantages of having a wolf-dog companion as a nomad in the wilderness are obvious, it's what happened *after* humans left this way of life that intrigues those of us who are curious about why and how we love dogs. "If you didn't need a working dog—and fewer and fewer people did,"

Kruger writes, "the ledger went out of balance. We kept paying dogs their food-and-shelter salary, but we got little that was tangible in return. Never mind, though; by then we were smitten."

Indeed we were. Indeed we *are*! Though not all people and not all cultures have loved and revered dogs as much as we do today, the fact that at least fifteen millennia have passed and we are still happily sharing food and beds with these animals tells us something about the depth of our love.

And that love doesn't only go one way. Though any dog owner will tell you that *obviously* our dogs love us back, thanks to the magic of MRIs, we now know this is true. Our dogs love us. One hundred percent. Science merely confirmed what our hearts already knew. And it's not just because those MRIs revealed that dog-brain "reward centers" light up more at the smell of a dog's favorite human than the smell of anything else. These MRIs have also revealed the extent to which dogs are attuned to our moods—and especially our suffering.

Consider this: researchers in one study found that "dogs were more inclined to approach a crying person than someone who was talking or humming, and that they responded to crying with submissive behavior. According to the researchers, this contrast indicates that the dogs' response to weeping wasn't simply the result of curiosity but was based on a primitive understanding of human distress. These findings indicate that when a dog comforts his sorrowful owner, the caregiver-recipient roles are sometimes reversed. The dog temporarily becomes the caregiver."

The next step was to test the theory. Again with the help of MRIs, dogs were trained to lie flat and get their brains scanned. The team found "increased activity in regions of their brain associated with attachment, empathy, and a theory of mind in response to their owners." This means that the dogs, when presented with the sounds or smells of their owners, would feel longing, concern, and even curiosity about them ("theory of mind" refers to what we wonder about). So while lying still during a brain scan, dogs were potentially worried and wondering about their beloved humans. Remarkable—not just in what it tells us about the dog-human relationship, but in what it tells us about love.

———

Part of why I thought I might not have always loved Jesus was most likely because I didn't understand love. Like most modern Americans, my idea of love—whether for family, partners, friends, children, or pets—is *romantic*. Not romantic meaning candlelight and roses (which would be disgusting, considering the list I just made), but meaning *emotional*. The Greeks famously had eight types of and words for love. We English speakers pretty much have one: one word and often just one understanding. We think of love as a *feeling*—and an overwhelming and specific feeling at that. When couples stop "loving" each other, it's really that they stop *feeling* love. Of course, it's heartbreaking when this feeling of love between partners dissipates. But I wonder sometimes whether our language of love—"I just don't love him anymore"—also reflects a limited view of love, one that narrows our vision. It's a view I once held.

While I understood that the feelings of love could change depending on the target (parents, dog, partner), I didn't understand just how deep and fierce love could be until I became a parent. Of course, every parent says something similar. And I understand that these words threaten to offend nonparents. I certainly used to feel this way before I had children. But as much as we love our partners, our parents, our nieces, our nephews, our dogs, our friends, our gods, we are biologically wired to love our kids in a whole different way. There's no way around this. And though I would have challenged this idea before I had kids, when I became a mom two decades ago, everything I thought I knew about love changed. It happened in two scenes: three days after my son Henrik was born, and before that, just moments after his birth. Let's start on the third day.

I fell head over heels in love with my firstborn on our second night home. As I nursed Henrik in the middle of the night, his eyes opened and met mine. For a few moments, they locked. It would be weeks (months?) before he would break a suckle to smile at me the dazzling way babies do, but as his hazel eyes met mine, they glimmered in the dark room. I was a goner. The rush of love came hard and fast. I was drowned in my head-over-heels-, shout-from-the-mountain-tops-, crazy-about-this-boy-ness.

But that was not the first moment I loved him. That happened just after Henrik was born, after first pulling his sticky body to my breast so he could nurse. I couldn't walk, due to a giant episiotomy and an epidural that managed to numb my legs but not the places that mattered. I was drained of energy—and nearly of blood—after eighteen hours of labor and nearly three hours of pushing. I was ravenous, thirsty, battered. But if anyone had tried to harm my baby in that moment, I would have ripped them apart with my bare hands or died trying.

That was my first moment of love. And *that* was when my understanding of the crazed, fierce, sacrificial love deepened. Thanks in part to the beauty of birth and to our animal friends.

———

The ferocity of mama grizzly bears is legendary. In fact, if fate has you scheduled for death by grizzly, it would most likely be because you stepped between a mama grizzly and her cubs. Some 70 percent of humans killed by grizzlies have made this same fatal, if usually accidental, mistake. But mama grizzlies aren't the only animals who show this fierce protectiveness of their children. You need only to be chased by the sharp honk of a mama goose at the park or spy the raised tail of a mama skunk marching her brood under a front stoop to understand that most animal moms are hardwired to fight hard to defend their young. Even the *flight* animals—those who turn tail at the slightest noise—eat their babies' placentas and then keep their babies on the move just moments after birth. If this doesn't show a badass fierceness and a do-anything desire to keep their babies safe, I don't know what does.

Though it's easy to chalk up these behaviors to instinct and be done with it, those who care about the word of God are challenged to look deeper and see that our instinct to love isn't merely a feeling. After all, again and again throughout the Scriptures, God describes the depth of God's love with metaphors from the animal kingdom. Consider the picture Deuteronomy 32:10–14 paints of God's protection and provision for God's people:

> He sustained him in a desert land,
>   in a howling wilderness waste;
> he shielded him, cared for him,
>   guarded him as the apple of his eye.
> As an eagle stirs up its nest,
>   and hovers over its young;
> as it spreads its wings, takes them up,
>   and bears them aloft on its pinions,
> the Lord alone guided him;
>   no foreign god was with him.
> He set him atop the heights of the land,
>   and fed him with produce of the field;
> he nursed him with honey from the crags,
>   with oil from flinty rock;
> curds from the herd, and milk from the
>   flock,
>   with fat of lambs and rams;
> Bashan bulls and goats,
>   together with the choicest wheat—

you drank fine wine from the blood of grapes.

Moses may not have had the sharpest of tongues, but if he is the author, he writes as well as he leads. Any lover of language will savor the brilliance of the images in this passage: howling wildernesses (come on!), honey from crags (yum!), and the blood of grapes (yes!).

But it's the image of God as Mama Eagle (or Mama Vulture, as some scholars say this should read) that stands out. In this passage, we imagine God hovering above a nest of eaglets, talons occasionally reaching down to "stir the nest"—which apparently implies plucking out the comfy bits and raising up the pokey parts, all to prepare the eaglets to leave the nest. We see God spreading her mighty wings, tucking her babies into her pinions, and carrying them off into the wind. God sets the birds on the heights and provides.

Nothing I've read tells me that eagles—or any birds of prey, actually—carry their babies on their wings like this, but that's not the point. Symbolism is our friend here. After all, Moses looks to one of God's most amazing creatures and one of the fiercest predators on Earth—one fully equipped with terrifying talons and powerful wings, with eyes that can spot the movement of prey from dazzling heights, and yet with an almost unmatched tenderness toward her young. All to show how much God loves us.

God loves as mama eagles love. Of course, God does it infinitely more, deeper, better—and all perfectly. God's love goes deeper than instinct. God's love is God's very essence. Perhaps this is why love *also* involves emotions and intentions. But our Creator set love deep into creation—so deep, in fact, that it comes out as instinct, something we don't need to think about—and made love *act* as well as *feel*. This is good news for all of us when we don't *feel* love. As long as we are offering care and acting in the best interests of another, we are loving them. As Bob Goff famously wrote, "Love does."

2

RESCUE

THE LORD IS MY SHEEPDOG

———◉———

"Who rescued who?" the popular bumper sticker and T-shirt slogan asks. The grammar may be wrong, but those of us who have adopted pets and know the hard-won joy of rescuing animals get it. The sentiment is right on.

Who rescued *whom* indeed.

Although humans—especially self-reliant American humans—don't like to speak of being rescued or (gasp!) *needing* rescue, animal rescues give us the language to talk about it. So, for instance, in the world of pet ownership, *adoption* means the rescue of an animal from a shelter or animal rescue organization. Though some people have started using *adopt* to include buying a pet from a breeder or from a pet store, pet adoption and pet purchase are not the same thing. Adoption fees cover rescue expenses and are never about profit.

The language we use matters.

"Who rescued whom?" gives us the language to speak to the two-way beautiful, saving work of rescue—for animals and people alike. So yes, we ask this question because we know or have experienced the story of the rescued therapy dog helping the soldier who once fought for others and who now fights her own PTSD. Or of the once abused, now "emotional support" dog who snuggles the child as he testifies against his abuser. Or, simply, of the rescued animals who offer comfort and presence in the darkest days or nights of the soul, who get us up and walking when getting out of bed is too much to manage.

Humanity's need for rescue—and desire to rescue others—runs from life-and-death situations to the getting-through-another-day sort. But people of faith are able to take this one step further. Because in going deep into animal rescue, we go deeper—straight, in fact—into the heart of God.

———

The sea otters dart behind the glass; their brown coats gleam silver as they slide through the water.

"It's Cooper and Watson!" I say. My hands clap in excitement. I can't believe I am looking at the sea otters in person. Though COVID-era attendance limits mean my family is the extent of their audience in this moment, in my mind, Cooper and Watson deserve vast applause. Not just because they enjoy a certain celebrity in their adopted hometown of Chicago—at least among those of us who care about animal rescue. But because of all they've been through, all they've overcome.

So I clap again and whisper to Cooper—or maybe Watson (who can tell?)—as he darts past, "I remember when you got here."

And remember I do. Long before the gift shop carried hoodies, tote bags, and T-shirts emblazoned with their back-floating likenesses, the two sea otter pups were found cold and alone on two separate Northern California beaches. Cooper was the healthier of the two, although as a lone sea otter pup with no mother in sight, his prognosis was still grim. Watson was in even worse shape. The wild Pacific surf had tossed and tumbled him, leaving Watson freezing, emaciated, and covered in sand. But some Good Samaritans got the pups to the Monterey Bay Aquarium, where vets and staff tended to them until Shedd Aquarium's animal response team could bring them to their permanent home in Chicago.

When Cooper and Watson arrived in Chicago, the oohs and aahs could nearly be heard around the city. News stations covered their journey. A contest was held to name them (they came in as Pups 870 and 872). More than twenty thousand people submitted suggestions.

With all the trouble in the world, it may seem silly that two rescued sea otters (or rescued koalas or ducklings or dogs, for that matter) can capture our hearts and compel people to submit name suggestions. Certainly, some people claim that "animal interest" stories serve only to distract us from more pressing people problems. But of course, it's precisely *because* the world is troubled and *because* people have problems that we get so invested in these rescues. Trying to participate in the rescue by sending donations or suggesting names for otters is in fact connected to our distress over the state of the world.

We love rescue stories—specifically animal rescue stories—because when lonely, tossed-and-tumbled sea otters are found, warmed, and fed, something about this troubled world clicks into place, if only for a moment. When we read of koalas being soothed and revived from wildfires or see ducklings scooped out of sewer drains, we are reminded that while this planet may be full of awful events and people, heroes exist.

When the world overwhelms us with heartache, seeing the terrified, emaciated pit bull pack on weight and overcome his fear of people is often just the reminder we need that people are still good. The brown pelican sometimes recovers from the oil spill. The dog doesn't always die at the end of the story.

But it's more than that, of course. As much as we don't like to admit it, rescue stories touch something deep within us because they speak to our own need to be rescued. No, we are not always weak or always in distress. We don't always need an intervention. But we do need help more often than we care to admit. True rescue involves so much more than just the one moment when the Good Samaritan scoops up the sea otter, the firefighter resuscitates the koala, the child reaches into the muck to grab the ducklings, or the rescue worker coos at the terrified pit bull.

Being rescued means being believed in, being worthy of a second (third, fourth, fifth . . .) chance. Being rescued means someone sees you and says, "No matter what, I'm not leaving you there—and I'm not leaving you like that." Rescue extends beyond the adrenaline-fueled moments. It involves planning, patience, and when done well, lots and lots of work.

In theological terms, to be rescued is to be saved, redeemed, justified, and sanctified. It's to be chosen, to be loved, to be shown mercy and grace. This is why the role of "rescuer" is central to who God is and "rescue" to what God does.

Once upon a time, I would have described the Bible as a "love story between God and God's people." I no longer say that. Besides sounding oddly romantic, that description lacks the blood-pumping action that courses throughout the Scriptures. And that action, of course, is God on a rescue mission.

Throughout the Scriptures—well, starting just three chapters in and then all the way through to the end—we watch God in motion, arms out, beckoning God's wandering people back. Whether God's people deliberately make a sharp-right and run or whether they slowly veer off the path, in the pages of this rescue mission, we see God's heart break. We feel God's blood pressure rise. And we see God get up from the throne and come on down to get God's people.

Of course, along the way, we also see God allowing consequences and correction. But throughout it all, the Scriptures thump and sizzle with God's rescuing presence. We see God offering guidance and extending mercy, and we hear God declaring again and again, "No matter what, I'm not leaving you there—and I'm not leaving you like that."

Of course, the biggest rescue story in Hebrew Scriptures isn't about animals at all (well, unless you count the frogs, the locusts, and the horses getting tossed into the sea, but according to the story, those poor horses hardly got rescued). In Exodus, we read of people who know they need rescue and get it. Though the rescue arrives after four hundred brutal years of enslavement, when God comes to the rescue, God *comes to the rescue.* We get the nervous and stuttering Moses uttering perhaps the most famous line in the Bible: "Let my people go." We get unbelievable (literally) plagues and miracles. God dazzles with might, leading the Hebrew people out of slavery and into a renewed covenant with God.

At the base of Mount Sinai, rescue takes new shape. Rescue moves into restoration. God has saved Israel, but God also intends to save the world through Israel's obedience and loyalty. So God provides the people with laws—ways to live in harmony with God and one another. And through their covenant relationship, God offers opportunities to redeem mistakes and receive fresh starts and new mercies. That doesn't go exactly as planned. The people disobey, wander off. But still, the rescue mission carries on, taking yet another shape. In it, we see different versions of God as rescuer.

One of the best things about the Bible is that it gives us so many pictures of God—many of them animals (more on this later). When it comes to God the rescuer, we get God as a roaring lion, as a swooping and saving eagle. But it's the image of God as an animal wrangler—as a good, rescuing shepherd, to be exact—that really gets my heart pumping. Maybe because I like sheep so much.

Of course, sheep are notorious for being stupid followers. Classic groupthinkers. Easy to coerce. Trouble is, this is all wrong. According to the BBC, "Sheep are actually surprisingly intelligent, with impressive memory and recognition skills. They build friendships, stick up for one another in fights, and feel sad when their friends are sent to slaughter." Their main fault is that they are "one of the most destructive creatures on the planet" and can deliver a mean kick when provoked.

We see why, with characteristics like these, sheep so often stand in for God's people in the Scriptures. Far from painting us as stupid followers, connecting us to sheep can mean that we are smart, capable of complex actions, loyal, and of course, destructive. And when we look at the characteristics of a shepherd—a good shepherd, at least—we understand why God claimed shepherd as a key role.

A shepherd's job description is fairly straight-forward: Care for and protect sheep. Guide them where they need to go. Obviously, there are a million more tasks, both menial and managerial (including, apparently, some business about fecal matter and flies around the tail). But that's the gist of the job. Though technology and markets have changed, as shepherding was millennia ago, so it essentially remains today. Which is super helpful for us! Because when the Bible teaches us about God as our good shepherd, we get it.

And those of us who love sheepdogs? We get it on a whole other level.

Though the instinct to flock together for protection is hardwired into sheep, smart and strong-willed sheep still do wander, especially if something startles them or they are led astray by a bad shepherd. This is where a good shepherd—human or canine—shines. At a sheep's first wander, a canine shepherd will spring into action. Imagine the black-and-white flash of a border collie against the green fields. The dog barks, circles wide around the rebel sheep, and closes in, routing it back toward the flock, toward safety.

Of course, that's the "easy" correction. A simple solution. Sometimes it's much more harrowing. Sometimes caring for sheep involves fighting off predators.

While border collies, Old English sheepdogs, and Australian shepherds round up the sheep, livestock guard dogs like mastiffs and Great Pyrenees have been bred to go growl-to-growl, fur-to-fur, and tooth-to-tooth with bears, wolves, and coyotes to protect the sheep. Sheepdogs risk their own well-being and lives—you could say that they lay down their lives—for the sheep.

Of course, human shepherds do the same, usually with weapons. But something about the sheepdog's responses speaks so beautifully to the nature of our good shepherd God. In fact, I was once so inspired by this image of God as shepherd that I imagined God as a German shepherd as I read through Psalm 23. I even wrote a children's book about it. I realize this type of metaphoric jump is not to everyone's taste. But since German shepherds guide and protect, cuddle and charge—and are loving, loyal, and brave to the core—the image holds.

Of course, the Scriptures give us the gorgeous language of God as an *actual human* shepherd. And not just because German shepherds didn't exist yet! David—a shepherd himself—calls the Lord *his* shepherd in the opening lines of the pastoral Psalm 23. It might lead us to wonder if it wasn't in fact David's own shepherd heart (rather than his raping and murderous heart) that God found to be "after God's own."

Then, four hundred or so years after David wrote about his shepherd-Lord, God gave Ezekiel this picture of God as shepherd:

> I myself will search for my sheep and look after them. As a shepherd looks after his scattered flock when he is with them, so will I look after my sheep. I will rescue them from all the places where they were scattered on a day of clouds and darkness. I will bring them out from the nations and gather them from the countries, and I will bring them into their own land. I will pasture them on the mountains of Israel, in the ravines and in all the settlements in the land. I will tend them in a good pasture, and the mountain heights of Israel will be their grazing land. There they will lie down in good grazing land, and there they will feed in a rich pasture on the mountains of Israel. I myself will tend my sheep and have them lie down, declares the Sovereign Lord. I will search for the lost and bring back the strays. I will bind up the injured and strengthen the weak, but the sleek and the

strong I will destroy. I will shepherd the flock
with justice. (Ezekiel 34:11–16 NIV)

Then, in the famous "Comfort, Comfort" passage (Isaiah 40:11 NIV), the prophet Isaiah gives us a
maternal view of God our shepherd:

He tends his flock like a shepherd:
He gathers the lambs in his arms
and carries them close to his heart;
he gently leads those that have young.

In the shepherd, we find one of the most complete
pictures of our tender, fierce, nurturing, and rescuing God.

———

Of course, even our stone-working Jesus took to the
image. In the parable of the lost sheep, Jesus shows us
the good shepherd leaving behind ninety-nine sheep
to rescue the one who has wandered away. Here, we
can practically see the lamb stuck in the crevice.
We can hear its pitiful *baas*, which turn into screeches
as the lion prowls and the vultures circle. It's a dangerous scene. A serious rescue mission.

And this, Jesus shows us, is what God does for us, what Jesus himself steps into. This story tells us why Jesus calls himself the good shepherd. Like all good shepherds—human, canine, or divine—Jesus says, he lays down his life for his sheep. For us. Because that's what rescue is all about.

Good shepherds don't just whistle and hope the sheep comes back. Good shepherds seek out the lost sheep. They go after them. Good shepherds don't just unsnag the sheep from the crevice. They don't just plop it back onto the hillside and run away. They look the sheep over. They scare away the predators. They carry it back to the flock. They bind its wounds and tend to it.

Good shepherds *risk* something in the rescue. Indeed, risk is part of rescue. Rescue is an inherently risky investment, putting yourself out there for the sake of another. Perhaps you've risked a relationship to confront a loved one about their addiction or troubling behavior. Perhaps you've struggled against rough waters to pull another to safety. Maybe you've adopted a terrified animal or transported a sea otter. However you have risked to rescue, you know: rescue comes at a cost. God sent God's Son. Jesus gave his life. But the reward? Lives are saved. God's people are welcomed back. Love grows.

That so many became invested in the lives of two tiny sea otters like Cooper and Watson means they also risked heartbreak. Had no one ever bothered to scoop them up, to warm them, to feed them, to fly them to Chicago, to submit a name, or to visit, no one's hearts would ever break for them. Now, on the day they die (may it be many years from now!), a city may mourn. Kids may cry. But the reward of having saved and loved will live on.

3

VICES
and
VIRTUES

HOW PIT BULLS CHOOSE TO LOVE

As a dog-walking volunteer, I should not have been in the kennel. And yet there I was, trapped between a snarling, drooling, jet-black pit bull and a cinder block wall.

As the dog barked and barked, I prayed and prayed. *Please. Help me get out of here.* I watched the dog's muscles flex under his fur. Sweat pooled on my palms. *This could end badly*, I thought. My time would be cut far too short. My tale would become yet another cautionary one.

Before I knew it, the dog settled for two seconds. I stepped over and around the dog and unlatched the kennel. I slid between the gate and yet another cinder block wall and latched the kennel closed.

I breathed deep. *Thank you, Jesus.* I squatted down and reached my fingers back through the cage.

"Sorry, buddy," I said. "But I wasn't supposed to be in there with you. Maybe next time, I can take you for a walk, and we can play." The dog licked my fingers and wiggled his butt and then went back to barking and jumping at the wild golden retriever across the way.

I once read that, like musical instruments and houses at Hogwarts, we don't choose our dogs. They choose us. And that sounds about right. After all, who knows why we're drawn to the dogs we're drawn to? But long before I loved a pit bull of my own—before I shared my bed and my lunch with the red-nosed Sierra or the brindled Vinny—that jet-black pittie whose name I never caught grabbed my heart.

Poor thing. He'd been picked up as a stray, locked up as so many pits are, scared, alone, hungry, thirsty. But in the three minutes I got myself trapped in his kennel, I realized something: though some might have seen his snarling and lunging at the dog across the way as *vicious*, I read his restraint toward me—his *temperance*—as *virtuous*. Could it be that these dogs, so maligned and so misunderstood, can teach us a thing or two about vices? And about virtues? And about the Creator who gave us a better way to live in a troubled world?

After all, pit bulls are almost certainly the most feared (read: hated) dogs around. But anyone who has known and loved a pit bull knows their secret. Far from ferocious, pit bulls are silly and snuggly, wonderful and wiggly. Though true that they were originally (and continue to be) bred to fight dogs, they were also bred to be "people passive." This means friendliness toward humans is a key attribute of pit bulls. This is true even of the ones who have lived lives of horror and abuse, those who have been neglected or made to fight. Countless numbers of these dogs go on to be the best family dogs. Despite what they've been through, even the most mistreated pit bulls trust and love their people although they have never been loved.

This is why I caved when I saw the jet-black pittie kick his bowl over as he wiggled his big butt and pawed at the kennel door, hoping for some love. He was alone and scared and thirsty, his voice hoarse from barking at that pesky golden retriever. I had to help.

But the police had just dropped him off as a stray. He'd not yet been evaluated by shelter staff. Thus, volunteers were not allowed in his kennel. I tried to reach his bowl with the long end of a pooper-scooper. I tried to find a nonswamped shelter worker to help. Both to no avail.

So I decided to break the rules. I'd get in and out of the kennel lickety-split, I thought. I'd done it a million times before with other dogs. Piece of cake.

The pit bull had been delighted to have me in the kennel—so delighted, in fact, that I got turned around resisting his jumpy kisses and full-body hugs. That was when the golden retriever across the way had had enough of our nonsense. The golden started barking again. Then, the pit. Their chaos threatened to blow my clandestine operation.

That was why I was scared in the kennel.

Never once did I think the wiggly pittie would hurt me. Never once did I fear he would turn those snappy teeth toward my hand or stomach or face or legs.

Granted, I am dangerously unafraid of dogs. I've clucked and cooed at K-9 German shepherds through police car windows while they lunged at the glass. I've fed and cuddled a neglected, chained-up, Rottweiler covered in his own poop. I've helped nervous police officers coax terrified and snarling strays out from under bushes. I've broken up fights involving my own dogs. (Pro tip: If you must break up a dogfight, never get between their teeth. Grab a fighting dog by its back legs.)

My three minutes in the kennel with the inky pit bull grabbed my heart, solidified my adoration for the type, and sparked something special about this dog, about *these* dogs. About pit bulls. Indeed, I wondered, What if what some see as vicious—that is, full of vice—could also be seen as virtuous? What if vice and virtue are two sides of the same sheet? What if what we perceive and judge as vices in others are sometimes actually virtues—just turned inside out or folded in a such way that we can't see the other side? Or what if vices aren't actual vices at all?

———

A virtue, according to the catechism of the Catholic Church, is a "habitual and firm disposition to do the good. It allows the person not only to perform good acts, but to give the best of [her or] himself. The virtuous person tends toward the good with all [her or] his sensory and spiritual powers; [she or] he pursues the good and chooses it in concrete actions."

Now, pit bulls may not have spiritual powers—at least not ones most churches would officially recognize. Plenty of people would argue that dogs don't make *moral* choices. But if you understand pit bulls, and if you believe that dogs do make *some* choices, this virtuous thing starts to make sense. Plus, if society believes a dog can be full of vice—and thus *vicious*—surely being full of virtue isn't much of a stretch.

After all, pit bulls as a type are mischaracterized and misunderstood to the point that they suffer brutality that's hard to stomach. Too many are starved, abused, neglected, and forced to fight. They are seen—at least by some—as "ticking time bombs," just moments away from ripping open someone's throat. They are banned from apartments, cities, counties, states, and entire nations (England!). One rapper calls himself Pitbull to appear tough and dangerous (although to me, it shows he must love to snuggle). Because of this, pit bulls die by the millions in shelters every single year, according to some.

And yet these dogs, who face so much misunderstanding and bigotry and cruelty, time and again seem to *choose* to show love. They *choose* to be loved, *choose* to trust, and *choose* to be trustworthy. Time and again, many pit bulls—to paraphrase the catechism—show a firm disposition for good. Despite all they have been through as a type and what so many have been through as individuals, these dogs give their best and do good. Where they could choose otherwise—mistrusting humans who have mistreated them—they *choose* to do good or are at least inclined to. That God put this resilience and ability to be and do good in the face of such trials tells us something about our Creator and also about these "rules" God set forth and placed deep in our hearts and into the heart of creation.

———

Virtues are full of problems. One, they're not nearly as fun as vices—to live, to read, or to write about. Best to get that truth out of the way right now. And two, they're hard to nail down. Different traditions, different church fathers, different Greek philosophers use all kinds of variations on the theme. Perhaps the most common set of virtues are the seven that combine the cardinal virtues with the *theological* virtues: prudence, temperance, justice, courage, faith, hope, and charity (love). Which leads to my biggest issue with virtues: the way church traditions—or perhaps "churchy pronouncements" is a better way to put it—have stripped virtues of their moxie and might. They seem so pure, so prim, don't they?

I once applied for a job with *Virtue* magazine. The magazine itself was terrific. It contained wonderful pieces about prayer, reading Scripture, and right living—orthodoxy, if you will—for women. But just as the very term *orthodoxy* has morphed from a broad position of correct Christian living to code for "you agree with a 'historic' view on same-sex marriage," so has the word *virtue* morphed: from bold characteristics that help us become like our mighty God (according to Saint Gregory of Nyssa) to something much softer, much more passive, much *safer*. That's why the vices are so much fun! We might even begin to assume that to live as a person of virtue is to live as a, well, boring person.

Let's be honest: when we imagine a *virtuous* person, we see a pure, kind, gentle *woman*. In my mind, she wears a wide-brimmed sun hat. She smiles broadly and brings great egg casseroles to the potluck brunch. She blesses everyone's hearts. In this—or in my—characterization, we've made the virtuous almost villainous!

Prudence, temperance, justice, courage, faith, hope, and *charity* may sound quaint, old-fashioned. But when you actually consider the attributes of the virtues—the meanings of the words—they are anything but. Virtuous people do not sit passively, fanning away the troubles of the world. Virtuous people do not faint in the face of adversity. They fight it. To live the virtues is to live boldly, to live fully, to live right. To be a person of virtue is to look straight at the troubles of the world, to bear them on your shoulders and deep in your soul, and to respond—not as the world does, but as pit bulls do.

Or perhaps less heretically, as Jesus does and as Jesus would have us do.

===

Just before Jesus launches into the parable of the Good Samaritan in Luke 10 (starting with verse 30), we witness a remarkable scene. An "expert in the law" asks Jesus what we must do to inherit eternal life. Luke tells us this question is a test. Noting this man's expertise, Jesus tosses the question back at him. "What is written in the law?" Jesus asks (Luke 10:26).

The expert echoes the words of Deuteronomy 6:5. "'Love the Lord your God with all your heart and with all your soul, and with all your strength, and with all your mind,'" he says. "'And your neighbor as yourself'" (Luke 10:27).

Allow me to paraphrase what happens next: Jesus gives the expert a thumbs-up. "Do that and you will live," Jesus says. And presumably, Jesus starts to move on, turning to another expert's question, perhaps. But this expert wants to justify himself, to prove his mind can stretch beyond the recitation of the Scriptures. So he puts up a finger and asks one more question: "Jesus, who *is* my neighbor?"

You can almost feel the ground shift under the weight of this question. Certainly everyone falls silent. You've got to believe Jesus smiles. This is a *good* question after all. Teed-up perfectly for Jesus, who came to toss everything—neighbor-love included—on its head. It's only after this that Jesus spins one of the greatest tales ever told: the parable of the Good Samaritan.

What I find most remarkable about this story—as with so many of Jesus's great stories—is not just the brilliance of the storytelling or the way he makes listeners squirm or burn with anger. Instead, it's how Jesus's stories *expand* the worldview of those who choose to believe them. This, of course, is a hallmark of all great stories. Just as novels increase our empathy toward the other, so do Jesus's parables and other stories expand our understanding of one another and how we're supposed to behave in this world.

In some ways, this was wildly unfair to the Pharisees, whom I always end up feeling bad for. After all, this group of experts had committed themselves to getting God's law right. And if you've read through the book of Leviticus, you know: God is *very* particular about God's law. The level of detail is astounding—in every meaning of the word. And the *consequences* for straying from the law are the stuff of nightmares. So wanting to keep these laws should be admirable.

But to Jesus, that wasn't the case. Because Jesus knew the point of the law wasn't mere obedience but that people should turn their hearts back to God and live as a light to other nations. The law that God gave the people was always more than a list of commands. It was about a way of life that was good for the people and good for others and that gave glory to God. The Pharisees seemed to miss that. So in his role of "fulfilling" the law, Jesus wasn't throwing it out but was opening it, warming it, taking it from the head to the heart, where it was meant to live all along.

The Pharisees had stripped the law of its fire, of its passion. They put the law in a box, on a pedestal, and feared it (sometimes in a good way, other times in a bad way). Somewhere along the line, they forgot to *live* it. And that's a point Jesus drove home by making the experts and priests the villains and casting a Samaritan as the hero.

And in the parable of the Good Samaritan, Jesus illustrates not only who our neighbors are (friends, enemies, anyone suffering, the oppressed) but also what loving our neighbors looks like. And of course, loving our neighbors often looks very much like living the virtues. After all, to show *prudence* is to show wisdom, discernment, practical sensibilities. To show *temperance* is to have restraint, self-control. To seek *justice* is to seek fairness and equality and to take a stand against selfishness. To show *courage* is to do the right thing in the face of danger. To show *faith* is to believe the unbelievable, perhaps even the laughable, about God or humanity. To show *hope* is to look to the best in even the worst circumstances. And to show *charity* is to love God, to love neighbors, to love enemies—and to be willing to sacrifice for the *good* of them all. That is how we live out the virtues. Those are not tame actions. That is not boring living.

———

I'm not going to lie: sometimes when I meet or read about a pit bull who escaped a life of horror and mistreatment to go on and show love beyond measure, I think of the Good Samaritan. The Samaritan was mistreated and maligned, considered a deplorable enemy of the Jewish people. He could have chosen the *vicious* path, that of the "experts" in the law, and left that man on the road to die. But he didn't. He chose good. He chose virtues despite the past, despite the present, despite the risk for the future—like the jet-black pittie in my cage.

There's a reason the Good Samaritan's story is told so often—and why I wanted to tell the story of the pittie. We only *think* the villains are more fun. (Well, sometimes maybe they are—to read and write about.) But the virtuous? Well, they change the world and help set things right in honor of our Creator.

4

DELIGHT

BUILDING HEDGEHOG HIGHWAYS

———◉———

First, the squirrel. Then, the fox.

Both raced across my lawn toward the huge crumbling ash tree in the parkway. The squirrel arrived first and scrambled straight up. Just a fox-length behind, the fox screeched to a halt, her front paws stretching up the trunk. I grabbed my phone and began filming just as the squirrel began a slow descent of the trunk.

I gasped. Was the squirrel *really* heading back down toward the fox?

The fox, not believing her luck, put her paws down on the ground and crouched. The squirrel inched closer and closer. Both fascinated and nervous, I put down my phone. I couldn't peel my eyes away. What was this squirrel thinking?

Just as the squirrel got within reach of the fox, the fox pounced. But the squirrel jerked to the right and circled back up the tree. The fox jumped and circled itself.

Then the action stopped—and repeated as the squirrel inched back down.

By this point, I was smiling at the squirrel's brazen outfoxing of the fox. The fox's sleek red body zipping around the ash tree made it easy to set aside any idea that the fox was looking for dinner or the squirrel was running for its life. Apparently, they were just having a good time. As I watched, their antics moved from fascinating and worrisome to nothing short of delightful—especially since the fox never did catch the squirrel and eventually stretched out on our neighbor's lawn for a nice survey of the street.

It doesn't take much to delight us animal lovers. We happily point out cows on road trips or bunnies in the park. We ask to pet every dog that walks by, and we seek out wildlife on neighborhood walks and in nature preserves and at the waterfront. All because animals—whether they're hunting or playing or grazing or just *being*—delight us. It's the promise of delight that makes us want animals to be part of our lives, whether in our homes or as neighbors on this planet.

———

To say a documentary about the bushfires that ravaged Australia and her wildlife in late 2019 and in 2020 "delighted" me sounds nothing short of cruel. Especially since the documentary featured footage of death, euthanasia, and terribly burned, frightened, orphaned, or starving animals as it followed the amazing rescuers who worked tirelessly to save some of the millions of animals killed in the bushfires.

Yet I'll say it: the documentary—*Nature*'s "Australian Bushfire Rescue"—amazed and delighted me. As poet Maxine Kumin writes in "Nurture," "I am drawn to such dramas of animal rescue. / They are warm in the throat." The animals of Australia have also delighted me since I was a child. Indeed, I'm not alone. These animals captivate children and adults alike—and for good reason. As a child, I'd flip through the pages of a book about Australia's wild and wonky animals and fantasize about cuddling koalas, beak-stroking platypuses, snuggling wombats, and hopping with kangaroos. I'd shiver over photos of deadly snakes and huge fruit bats. Still, my wonder over the other animals kept my nose deep in that book and delighted me for days. As Sy Montgomery writes in her book *How to Be a Good Creature*, "Sculpted by isolation, Australia's animals outpace the imagination."

So while this documentary about the demise of animals that I'd spent a lifetime dreaming about broke my heart, the stories of people committed to *saving* them lifted my spirits. Despite the struggle of those that survived, often either orphaned or wounded, the footage of these feisty creatures rising from literal ashes heartened me. This story of the fight, moxie, and amazingness of Australia's animals unfurled delight after delight after delight.

How could watching a dedicated family of rescuers bottle-feed joeys or researchers set up cool-water-spritzing systems for fruit bats (yes, fruit bats!) not be delightful? How could we not smile as we watch human foster moms snuggle orphaned wombats? How could we not ooh and aah over two orphaned joeys hugging or two wombats waddling and wandering as rescuers prepare them for release into a burned-down wild?

After all, no longer were these animals of Australia delightful simply because of their marsupialness or their mixed-and-matched parts or their exotic charms. Now they delighted us because in each step, snuggle, and suckle, they were beating the odds. They were putting their trust in humans to help them, and they were showing the world that we humans can and must do better in protecting their habitats and ability to thrive.

But that's the thing about animals, about noticing and delighting in them. We can delight in their steps forward and successes. We can delight in their silliness and hard work. We can delight in their appearance and in their sounds. We can delight in the ways we can help them—and in how they help us.

In fact, pay enough attention to the animals in this world, and you'll find not only endless reasons to delight in them; you'll learn what it means to delight and to be delighted in. This, in turn, helps us understand the way our Creator feels about creation—and us. If we believe the Scriptures, these animals we love—from the plunky platypus to the dog on our lap—can also help us understand how we are to feel about God.

———

If you search for the word *delight* in the Bible, you'll find the Scriptures talk a surprising amount about delight. Like, a *lot*. Through Psalms, Proverbs, Esther, Isaiah, and the Prophets, through the Gospels and the Epistles, we read again and again about God delighting in us, us delighting in God, people delighting in people, and people delighting in obeying the law (of all things!). Scripture writers wonder about what delights God and how we can delight in God. All that delight is delightful, really. And it's too often overlooked. Delight rarely shows up on lists of important theological words—at least none that I've come across.

Maybe that's because *delight* can sound shallow somehow, or childish. But of course, when we understand what delight is, we discover it's anything but. *Delight* is a terrific word—and an even better feeling. Consider how one writer describes what happens when we experience delight: "When something surprises you, your brain immediately drops what it's doing and gives your full attention to the thing that surprised you. This is largely a survival instinct—if something jumps out from the bushes, your body primes you to respond to it. As a result, surprises amplify the emotional effect of whatever you experience next, good or bad. . . . So in essence, delight is a brief moment of concentrated joy, made possible by the compounding element of surprise."

And so delight—this "moment of concentrated joy"—sparkles yet runs deep. Delight tickles our fancy (*fancy* being shorthand for the brain's pleasure center) and permeates our spirits. Though delight is necessarily surprising and often momentary, it is not fleeting, and it can be sought. Delight lingers long after an encounter and leaves us longing for more. We want to delight and be delighted. *And* we want to share our delightful experiences with others.

Certainly this is why the Scriptures speak so much about delight. Delight is both motivation and reward. Delight is something we can both experience and offer. We can both delight *in* the Lord and delight *the* Lord. In many ways, delight, rooted in love, is the essence of a good relationship with God.

Consider this: the psalmist tells us that if we delight in the Lord, the Lord will give us the desires of our hearts. It would be nice if this meant God was a genie in a bottle and indulged our every whim and fancy when we delighted in God. But I can't imagine this is what this verse means—at least, not regularly. It makes more sense that this is a deeper dive into *lasting* delight. If so, then the psalmist is assuring us that when we find our delight in God, God puts desires—longings, dreams, and goals—in our hearts. Then, in living out or seeking those God-given desires, we in turn delight God, and round and round we go. Delight upon delight upon delight.

But this still doesn't help us understand *how* we delight in God—perhaps especially when times are tough and we barely believe in God. Even when times are good, delighting in rescued wombats on TV—or in the squirrels that race and chase through my backyard—is one thing. But delighting in our Creator the way we might delight in a wombat? How do we manage that?

———

Perhaps a hedgehog highway can help. Hedgehogs, of course, are prickly little roly-poly creatures. Think smaller and much less dangerous porcupines capable of curling into tiny balls at the hint of fear. Hedgehogs are found across Asia and Africa, but thanks to Beatrix Potter, hedgehogs are, in my mind, the most fascinating and beloved beasts of the English countryside.

Perhaps this is why, despite COVID travel restrictions and a simmering anger at the United Kingdom's continued pit bull bans, reading about England's miles and miles and miles of "hedgehog highways" had me looking at flights. These I need to see. After all, the highways are, apparently, "an eccentric delight—stone steps, hedgehog cutouts and little signs like 'Church' for any hedgehog that can read."

But these hedgehog highways, which weave through countrysides and through gardens and into churchyards and past pubs, aren't there merely for kicks. They are saving the lives of England's hedgehogs, whose numbers have decreased more than 90 percent since World War II. By giving the hedgies places to mate and wander, away from dangerous roads, organizations like Hedgehog Street are making safe paths for the little mammals. Encouraging people to cut small hedgehog holes in fences and then mark the holes with a fun sign so the holes don't get covered up creates new highways for the hedgehogs to traverse and meet with mates.

This alone is an admirable act. Knowing you are helping save an amazing creature like the hedgehog should be reward enough. But, it turns out, the result of seeing hedgehog poop in your garden or seeing one tramp down your ramp or knock over the twigs you left to see if your highway got used—well, it is complete delight, delight, and more delight. In fact, this is the kind of delight that comes not from pure surprise or serendipity but from a "Hey, it worked!" kind of surprise. In other words, when you prepare for but don't expect a lovely surprise to happen, delight results.

It's in *this* way that we learn to delight in God. Just as God prepares ways in the wilderness for us and promises to light our paths, so too can we prepare highways for God to make God's way into our lives. When we do this—when we actively construct ways to experience God—we can't help but delight in God.

These highways for God are found in reading the Scriptures, in praying, in seeking silence, in practicing gratitude and other disciplines, and in seeking God's will, as the psalmists repeatedly found. But more than anything, I find that we build hedgehog highways for God when we simply live with our eyes and ears open, with all our senses alert, with an expectation that God will ramble through the holes we've chiseled and down the ramps we've built. Then we will find God among us, in the garden of our lives—even if we have trouble believing in God or God's goodness.

This is not to say the element of surprise is gone when it comes to delighting in God. God can and does surprise us, just as hedgehogs do. Isabel Houselander, a ten-year-old British girl interviewed for an article about hedgehog highways, believed hedgehogs were imaginary creatures—until she saw one on her garden camera. The acts and preparation of those who built the hedgehog highways actually helped her believe.

I have great sympathy for her skepticism. My own city-reared husband thought reindeer were made-up Christmas creatures until we saw them at the zoo on one of our first dates. As we approached the pen and he read the sign, he gasped in delight and said, "I didn't think they were real!" It was as if we'd run into Santa Claus.

But here's the thing about delight and God: we can build on-ramps to find God delightful (and thus, also delight God), but God also delights in thrilling *us*, surprising *us*, and delighting *us* in God's creation, just because. God actually prepares the highways for us to encounter God and all God's delights. This is why pink-striped skies at night take our breath away. It's why we hold our hands out before mountains and waves. It's why we stop and bend to admire wild-flowers. It's why we pause to watch squirrels. And when we open our senses to it, we see this is God all around, with us.

God set delight right into creation. I like to imagine that as God dreamed up and set plans in motion for pokey little roly-poly hedgehogs, God knew they would delight humans as much as they delight God. And perhaps God even saw that when hedgehogs needed saving, it would be our delight in them that would come to the rescue and be the reward.

5

ADAPTABILITY

COYOTES ON THE REBOUND

———————◦———————

The slim gray animal darts across my lawn. I stand up and lean deeper into the bay window.

"Oh no! A lost dog!" I say out loud. To myself. No one is around. It slinks into my neighbor's bushes as a man and his dog walk across the street. Only then do I realize my mistake—the same one I always make.

That is no lost dog. *That* is a coyote. The man and his dog don't even know it's there, hiding in the bushes, watching and waiting till they are safely gone to resume its neighborhood prowl. Such is the way of coyotes.

But I have my ways as well. So I watch the beautiful animal for a few minutes from my own sneaky spot, smiling as I do. Because spying on this legendary and (wrongly) feared wildlife from the comfort of my bay window in the suburbs is something I never thought I'd enjoy.

I live in the town where I grew up. For all of my growing-up years—the 1970s, '80s, and '90s—and then beyond that, into the 2000s, coyotes were not a thing. They did not live in the near-west suburbs of Chicago. Coyotes were the kind of animal that *used* to roam these parts, before the suburban sprawl obliterated their habitats and tightened their roving territories.

But then suddenly—or so it seemed—they came back. And not just to the suburbs, with their forest preserves, spots of reclaimed prairie, and creek-side paths that meander through the towns. No, they came back into the city—into Chicago. Today, wild-life experts believe there are about four thousand coyotes living in Chicago and the surrounding suburbs. This number has doubled in the past fifteen or so years.

Though plenty of people worry about the coyotes—neighbors on community connection websites routinely post warnings of coyote sightings—most have now become coyote champions. We share sightings of the shy (and harmless to people and large pets) animals to celebrate their recovery. We revel in their beauty and affirm that comebacks—resurrections, even—still happen.

Though at first their reappearance was perplexing, we now understand that our community and the city just a few miles east of us offer coyotes a hunting-free haven. And we realize that this haven is replete with a coyote's favorite foods: geese, bunnies, and squirrels.

I'll admit it: I have fallen hard for coyotes. As much as our current neighborhood fox delights me, I mourn that foxes and coyotes don't share territory. So when I see the fox, I grieve, knowing the coyotes no longer call my neighborhood home.

Coyotes are not hard to fall for. Beautiful and stealthy, they are positively swoon-worthy. Unlike foxes, who streak brazenly through side yards and whose siren-red fur demands attention, coyotes slink and sneak. They are neighborhood ghosts, roaming, lurking, and living among us without being seen unless they want to be.

I love coyotes for all these reasons, but mostly I love them because they came back. Because they restaked their claim to this land. Because they took a look at these crowded suburbs and that bustling city, saw that they were still home to all their favorite foods, and said, "This'll do just fine."

With each warning a scared neighbor posts, reminding us that coyotes once again live among us, we remember that the creatures of this world were made to adapt, to adjust, to carry on. And those of us who recognize God's hand at work in the world see that these creatures' ability to adapt to the new, the different, and even the terrible reveals God's hand.

Obviously, creation and creatures have suffered terribly—to the point of extinction or nearly so—at the hands of humans. Our good God weeps over how poorly we have stewarded this world. But with every creature that adapts and rebounds, we see the goodness of God pour over creation—and see creation benefit from it.

━━━━━

The Garden of Eden with the Fall of Man by Peter Paul Rubens and Jan Brueghel the Elder is a most troubling painting. Not because of the technique or anything to do with actual art. Nor because it depicts Eve handing Adam the fruit, nor because we're looking into the last moments of "perfection" in creation.

No, it's troubling because even though this painting shows the scene before the fall, Adam and Eve are surrounded by and even themselves display signs of sin. First of all, Ruben and Brueghel's Adam and

Eve have red hair. As my science-y, brown-haired, brown-eyed daughter has happily told me—her blonde-haired, green-eyed mother—many times, I am a genetic mutant, as are my redheaded friends. Black or dark brown hair and brown eyes are the standard from which the rest of us deviate. Of course, these white European artists wouldn't have known this circa 1615. But if we believe God created a perfect world, it seems unlikely our first ancestors were tainted, mutant gingers.

Second of all, the painting shows dogs crouching in full "play bows," leaning down on their elbows with their front legs out. Although the black and brown dogs look like pit bull ancestors, which absolutely delights me, should there be *dogs* in the garden of Eden? Hardly. Dogs didn't exist until ten thousand or so years ago. That's when scientists guess the first friendly wolf wandered up to humans for fire, food, or company. And that's when early humans tossed the first bit of venison and made room in beds for those fluffy, wolfy dogs to snuggle up. The world was full of people by this point, long past the garden of Eden.

But mostly, the painting is troubling because the other animals in the painting reveal adaptations, traits that developed through generation upon generation to help animals hunt or hide better—that is, to survive. Why would they have needed help surviving before the fall? Isn't that the orthodox view of when death entered the world?

Consider some of the creatures we see front and center in the painting. While certainly God may have created macaws with bright feathers just for God's delight, scientists tell us that macaws developed bright feathers to attract mates *and* to help themselves hide from predators among bunches of equally bright rainforest flowers. While God may have given goats tough hooves and horns simply because God likes their click and clack, scientists tell us goats evolved with hooves and horns to fight off predators. And while God could have given the tiger her stripes and the leopard her spots just to mix it up a little, scientists tell us tigers and leopards developed these marks to hide and better surprise their prey. They are stripy and spotty so they can pounce quicker and kill better.

Of course, we see this painting with an understanding of science and a theological perspective these seventeenth-century artists did not share. Those of us who look at it today can note that some aspects seem odd for a painting depicting a time before death entered the world and in which animals and people lived in peace together. You can see why the painting is troubling, theologically speaking. It makes us take a new look at what we may have long believed about the garden days.

And yet the painting is also touching, because the artists reveal a deep longing, something we all want and need to believe. That is, we hope that our mutations, our callouses, our scars, our gray hairs, our muscle-and-grit—our *anything* that's been developed through the push and pull and the terrors and trials of life—make us interesting. These are the adaptations that make us *us* and that make us good, very good, in the eyes of God.

═══

This is not to say adaptability is bad—or that it only entered the world after sin did. Of course, some people believe this is true, particularly those who discount what scientists tell us about the origins of this world. Plenty of folks would never see any issue with Rubens's painting. *Of course tigers were created exactly as such—with stripes and everything!* And sure, they could be right. God could have created each animal with stripes and spots and feathers just for God's delight and glory. Perhaps it was only after death entered the world in a new way that God allowed those delightful, glorious characteristics to serve double duty.

God could have done this, just as God could have created the world in six twenty-four-hour days—three of which happened before there was a setting and rising sun. God could have created the earth less than ten thousand years ago and only made the world *look* old. God could have done this to trick geologists, biologists, zoologists, botanists, physicists, astronomers, and all the other scientists whose research points to a much older universe. It seems quite unlikely—and unlike the God I know—but sure, God could have done all this for kicks.

Or our *good* God could have made people and animals and plants and minerals and atoms good—*very* good, in fact—and allowed our ability to adapt to carry on after death and sin came into play. God could have done this as part of a rescue plan or simply because the ability to adapt is *itself* a very good thing.

The way I see it, creation's ability to adapt is both a sign of God's rescue plan *and* part of our goodness. After all, I believe God created through evolution, that God drew one good being out of another. Perhaps because I'm a writer and am comfortable in the world of evolving ideas, or perhaps because I love the image of God as a potter who transforms matter and beings, evolution doesn't worry me. It doesn't detract from my image of a creator God, nor does it mess with my idea of humans or trouble my reading of the creation story.

In fact, our ability to adapt only enhances my view of our Creator and creation and of how God sees us. This might be what Rubens and Brueghel were getting at. Perhaps the truth is that our adaptations, our mutations, *are* our perfections.

Certainly, even today, with all we know about evolution and adaptation and mutation, if you were asked to paint or write a picture of Adam naming the animals, few of us would paint birds or lizards or wild cats with no camouflaging markings. Few of us would paint only the most primitive creatures in the garden. Most of us would create images of animals as we know them today—full of adaptations, developed by imperfection, which somehow lead to a new kind of perfection. It's complicated. It's confusing. But it's so like God to do.

———

Our ability to adapt—all creatures' ability to adapt—is what is so, so good about this world. And our ability to change and adjust in response to our trials and troubles reflects what is so, so good about our Creator. When I see the coyote scooting through my yard, I'm tempted to raise hands in praise. Humans have done so much damage, but God is so good. By setting adaptability into creation, God can turn humans' greed into good.

Of course, adaptation has its negatives. That is, creatures can adapt negatively; we can adapt in ways that don't help future generations at all. Trauma can be passed down through DNA. Humans sometimes "adapt" to pain by taking on all sorts of vices. The dog-breeding world is replete with examples of this. Baby bulldogs are born via C-section because mama bulldog birth canals haven't adapted to the size of their offsprings' heads. Breed-specific illness and dysfunction run rampant. (I must pause to say: Spay and neuter your pets. Adopt; don't shop.)

We know not every creature fares so well on the adaptation scale. Dinosaurs didn't. According to a report from the World Wildlife Fund, humans have wiped out 60 percent of the animals on Earth since 1970. Some scientists believe humans have killed off 83 percent of animals since the world began and that it would take five to seven million years to recover.

These stats shake me to the core. I was born in 1972. In my lifetime, my Earth-mates and I have wiped out 60 percent of the world's animals. How could this be? What have we done? What *can* we do? I don't say this often, or lightly, but when I read stats like the ones in the previous paragraph, "Lord, come quickly" spills out of my mouth. Anti-environmentalists use this phrase as an excuse to terrorize the planet. I say it recognizing the need for God to restore this planet to its full, intended glory. But saying these words also opens my eyes to the ways God is already at work. And God is.

We have much to repent for as humans. The things we have done—and continue to do—are unconscionable. And yet the animals that come back, that resist, that *adapt*? These creatures reveal God's hand— a hand that turns terror into triumph, suffering into sanctification, and grit into glory.

Adaptability is so deeply written into the brilliant design of things that to imagine a tiger without her stripes—just a standard yellow thing with no need to blend to defend—is to lose the glory of the tiger. To imagine a mountain goat without literal ass-kicking hooves and horns? That is to lose the glory of the mountain goat. To imagine the macaw without his sneak-into-the-flora feathers is to lose the glory of that bird.

In God's goodness, the adaptations we develop to survive *become* our perfection—or at least reflect the perfect design of our Creator. So much so that poet James Dickey imagined that in heaven, animals would be perfected in their predator and prey status. In "The Heaven of Animals," Dickey describes a place and time where animals wouldn't lose their drive to hunt—or to hide. Instead, predator *and* prey would revel fearlessly in heaven's perfected state.

In his view of heaven, Dickey writes it could not *be* a perfect heaven "without blood." Dickey then offers a picture of predators hunting with "perfect" claws and teeth and of prey being hunted, falling, and rising again. It's gorgeous—and rings true and full of hope. I love the idea that we take our adaptations, our mutations, and our scars to "heaven," where they are redeemed. I love that Dickey's picture of heaven asks how perfect a tiger can be if she cannot stalk and pounce, if she cannot sink her face in the blood of another as a means of caring for her young. I love that Dickey's picture of heaven asks how an antelope could be the perfect antelope if it can't spring fast and flee from predators. And I love that Dickey's picture of heaven involves a good God who set adaptation into creation—and allows the things that *could* destroy us to instead shape and fuel and propel us. I love that Dickey maintains we carry these things into a new, perfect eternity.

Of course, this view of heaven is confusing, as are all views of heaven. So perhaps this is just as theologically troubling to some as the painting was to me. Or perhaps this is what Rubens and Brueghel were painting all along. After all, our adaptations and mutations—our stripes, our bright feathers, our sleek shapes, our sharp fangs—make us good, very good.

6

GUT INSTINCT

TO PUT YOUR SNOUT TO THE SKY

On December 26, 2004, the tsunami roared in like a freight train, sucking the shoreline water back to power waves that reached fifty feet, according to some sources. *National Geographic* described it this way: "Giant forces that had been building up deep in the earth for hundreds of years were released suddenly on December 26, shaking the ground violently and unleashing a series of killer waves that sped across the Indian Ocean at the speed of a jet airliner. By the end of the day, more than 150,000 people were dead or missing and millions more were homeless in 11 countries, making it perhaps the most destructive tsunami in history."

We watched the footage in horror. Phone cameras captured the waters rushing past hotels, up hillsides. The horrors only increased as the tickers rolled across our screens, containing the numbers of people drowned, crushed by debris, or slammed into structures.

Then other stories began to emerge. According to local sources and lore, animals seemed to have escaped the devastation. Even though the waters rushed nearly three kilometers inland at Yala National Park, the largest wildlife reserve in Sri Lanka, in the immediate aftermath, *no* animals were found dead. None. Elephants, rabbits, and birds had headed for higher land ahead of the catastrophe.

A miracle.

"Animals can sense disaster," said H. D. Ratnayake, deputy director of Sri Lanka's wildlife department. "They have a sixth sense. They know when things are happening."

You don't have to be a wildlife expert to see that animal instincts go beyond the earthiness of eating birth sacs and placentas and marking territory and right into the realm of the otherworldly—or so it seems. When animals respond to nature—when animals *sense things happening* in ways we cannot, at least not without technology—they remind us that our Creator "set eternity in the human heart"

(Ecclesiastes 3:11 NIV). Unlike our creature friends, we humans do not have instincts finely honed enough to sense unseen warnings of disaster in the natural world. But like them, we were made to connect with this world, to respond to this world, and to experience God through this world.

═══════

My childhood was accompanied by dogs who spun in their beds to find just the perfect spot, who dug holes to nowhere, and who began to quake long before thunderclouds rolled in. I spent hours watching squirrels tuck acorns into various nooks and dirt patches in the yard. And no vacation was complete without noting—and asking questions about—the weird things the local animals did. (These things all still happen in my adulthood, by the way.)

As all lifelong animal lovers can attest, growing up watching animals helps you understand and appreciate that animals behave in certain ways out of *instinct*.

Still, I probably would have gone well into adulthood without thinking too deeply about animal instincts were it not for a certain episode of the *Muppet Show* that aired in what seems like another lifetime—1978. That was when I sat, rapt, watching a Muppet possum sing out a warning to terrified woodland Muppets. Muppet hunters were on the move, wandering through their woods with rifles. Today I watch the skit and recoil at some objectionable cultural stereotypes, and today I understand the nuances of hunting (that can be ecologically helpful and humane). But back then, I saw it differently.

As I listened to the possum sing rewritten lyrics to Buffalo Springfield's "For What It's Worth" and command the creatures to "stop . . . children. What's that sound? Everybody look what's going 'round," something deep within my six-year-old soul was moved. My young conscience was convinced of two things. One: hunting for kicks and giggles is evil. And two: the instincts that animals possess—in this case, sensing danger—are mysteries worth paying attention to.

I still believe both these things. Because what we see in the Muppets skit echoes something very real about instincts. By definition, an *instinct* is an unlearned response to a stimulus. Yet the true meaning goes so much deeper than muscle memory or movement. In many ways, instincts are magic. Instincts are miracles. Instincts are prophetic.

Far from being simple reactionary measures, animal instincts reveal a deep connection to the physical and spiritual world. The ability to both *sense* and *respond* to what is coming is a gift to be envied. To put your snout to the sky and sense a change in the weather or mood—and then to be able to adjust, respond, and react—is to save lives. To sense danger and then respond to it is to save the world.

I wish humans had more of this instinctual sensibility. I also wonder if we actually have more of this than we realize. It's not enough to say that God gave animals instincts and gave humans the ability to think creatively and originally and emotively. After all, animals can do that too. Many animals problem solve. Many animals grieve. *All* animals feel. And of course, humans also rely on instinct. A newborn turns toward a breast and roots for nourishment just moments after first breath. We rub our hands together when we're cold. And any parent who's ever stopped short in the car with a kid in the passenger seat knows we do not think before throwing an arm across our child. We just do.

Likewise, to live through 2020, with the start of pandemic shutdowns, is to have experienced the ultimate "hunkering down" instincts. During this year, we stocked up on toilet paper and learned to bake sourdough bread—so much so that it became a meme and a joke. And yet these instincts to gather and nest and provide during times of uncertainty are not necessarily things we learn (though perhaps for some of us they are). They are longings that arise when prompted by certain stimuli.

But so often we want to override our instincts or belittle them. We're uncomfortable knowing that parts of ourselves operate beyond our control—when actually *most* of ourselves operate without control. We do not think to breathe or pulse blood through our veins. Our stomachs grind and our bodies shiver without ever being told. All instinct. And all worth paying attention to. Like the animals do.

So, we might try to stop, children, and say, "What's that sound?"

———

Years ago, I asked a friend who founded and runs a very large social service agency in Chicago what she does when people ask for money on the streets. I expected her response to be precise—perhaps listing when, how, and *what* to give. Instead, she half-shrugged and said, "Let it be Spirit-led."

This was the greatest advice, the best wisdom I'd ever heard—about giving to those asking, but really, about anything. Just as we don't love listening to our instincts, doing anything "Spirit-led" feels awkward to most people. It's just so ooky-spooky and unpredictable. The trouble with listening to or acting upon the Spirit is that we could be *wrong*. Or it might be *hard*, or at least uncomfortable. And yet listening and responding to the Spirit is an instinct on par with—or better than, really—pulling our hands back from a hot surface or hugging our crying child. Of course, this kind of instinct requires some learning and practice, which probably makes it *not* exactly an instinct and more like spiritual muscle memory, which is pretty close.

After all, we—all creatures, I believe—were made to listen not only to our guts and our instincts but to the Spirit. And the Spirit is at work in our conscience (you could call it the "gut" of our psyche) whether we recognize her or not. When the writer of Ecclesiastes—that great book full of big sighs and shoulder shrugs—tells us God "set eternity" (Ecclesiastes 3:11 NIV) into our hearts, it's a reminder that while we may not understand or see the "time for everything" (Ecclesiastes 3:1 NIV) around us, we were made to contemplate it.

Paul tells us in Romans 2:13–15 that it's "not the hearers of the law who are righteous in God's sight, but the doers of the law who will be justified." The apostle adds, "When Gentiles, who do not possess the law, do instinctively what the law requires, these, though not having the law, are a law to themselves. They show that what the law requires is written on their hearts, to which their own conscience also bears witness." This is remarkable. Laws of goodness—of loving our neighbor—are written on our hearts. They're instinctive!

And the prophets show pictures of God's broken heart when we do not heed the instincts that lead us to God. The prophet Isaiah writes,

Hear, O heavens, and listen, O earth;
for the Lord has spoken:
I reared children and brought them up,
but they have rebelled against me.
The ox knows its owner,
and the donkey its master's crib;
but Israel does not know,
my people do not understand. (Isaiah
1:2–3)

In Jeremiah, we read,

You shall say to them, Thus says the Lord:
When people fall, do they not get up again?
If they go astray, do they not turn back?
Why then has this people turned away
in perpetual backsliding?
. . .

Even the stork in the heavens
    knows its times;
and the turtledove, swallow, and crane
    observe the time of their coming;
but my people do not know
    the ordinance of the Lord. (Jeremiah
    8:4–5, 7)

Just as God gave birds an instinct to migrate—to turn tail and fly another direction—so has God given us a longing to turn to God, to seek the Spirit, and to turn toward the *good*. Somewhere along the line, we've gotten good at burying or denying this instinct rather than cultivating it.

————

When I was a girl—the same age I was watching the *Muppet Show*—my dad and I participated in a father-daughter YMCA group called Indian Princesses. Of course, this group exhibited cultural appropriation (racism, really) at its worst. It seems it would also be sexist—except, aside from being gender-specific in membership, the activities were hardly "girly." Anyway, if 1970s "well-meaning" appropriation has a redemptive feature, it's that this group fostered a deep love and appreciation for Native American culture—at least, as it was presented. The love and worship of nature, particularly by the deeply religious Hopi, resonated with me, at that time, a baptized (though already questioning) Lutheran girl.

When I worried when people spoke of Jesus being the "only way" to heaven, my mother encouraged me to understand that a desire to worship the sun—or any wild weather—was simply a reflection of our innate desire to worship something more powerful than ourselves. Who knows, she'd say, how the Holy Spirit was speaking to the Hopi through the sun and through the storm clouds?

In some ways, I do know—because God has always spoken to me that way too. While I have what could be considered heterodox views on the bigness and mercy of God, these early wonderings and concern for what or *whom* we worship has long made me a believer in a human instinct *to* worship. Of course, neuroscientists back me up here—for much more skeptical reasons.

According to journalist Brandon Ambrosino, neuroscientist Andrew Newberg, who studies the brain and religions, contends that religious experiences "satisfy two basic functions of the brain: self-maintenance ('How do we survive as individuals and as a species?') and self-transcendence ('How do we continue to evolve and change ourselves as people?')."

Newberg also contends that spiritual practices and rituals blur the boundaries between ourselves and God ("or whatever it is you feel connected to") and we feel "one" with God or our higher power.

Other researchers say this feeling is nothing more than our Hypersensitive Agency Detection Device—or HADD—at work. HADD is a "nonreflective" evolutionary belief every mammal is equipped with. Ambrosino describes HADD this way:

> Say you're out in the savannah and you hear a bush rustle. What do you think? "Oh, it's just the wind. I'm perfectly fine to stay right where I am." Or, "It's a predator, time to run!" We may conclude it's just the wind and stay put. Or, we may conclude it's a predator and "time to run!" Well, from an evolutionary perspective, the second option makes the most sense. If you take the precaution of fleeing and the rustling ends up being nothing more than the wind, then you haven't really lost anything. But if you decide to ignore the sound and a predator really is about to pounce, then you're going to get eaten.

When explaining what makes us reach for a god or religion, still others, according to Ambrosino, point to the endorphin-releasing benefits of religious practices and thus see religion as community-wide "endorphin-triggering activation."

I'll be honest: reading the science behind *why* our brains respond to religion and God does nothing to minimize my faith. It only affirms it. I don't fret that God would use our own biology—by employing endorphins, for example—to move us toward God. Plenty of Christians think scientists who study the biological roots of spirituality are dismissing faith as part of their research. But when I look at what those scientists tell us, I only see a God who made all us creatures to seek and respond to God in this world. That our animal brains can respond this way is humbling and amazing.

And rather than brushing off our spiritual or faith "instinct" because there *is* a biological element, we should work toward cultivating this instinct. After all, this happens in the animal world too. Animals' instincts to react and respond make them deeply connected to the physical world—and, I'd argue, to the spiritual world. The same goes for us.

———

The back door creaked open and then slammed shut. I looked over at my dog. Snooze. Snore. Snore some more. Though I knew it was the sound of my son returning, my dog certainly didn't. It could've been someone coming to rob or murder us in that deep darkness of the early winter evening.

But as a pit bull, Vinny has an instinct to trust people (and to get plenty of sleep!). This is in stark contrast to the Rottweiler we had years ago. The Rottie trusted no one—that is, until they were squarely in the house or yard and he could see that they were accepted by us. But as long as a person was on the *other* side of the window, wall, door, or gate, they were bad news. So, the barking and growling commenced. No door would have ever opened in my house without that dog bounding and barking out of bed. Bark first, greet later.

Both pit bulls and Rottweilers are "bully breeds"—a term I have very mixed emotions about. Most people think they are both guard dogs and share similar instincts. This could not be further from the truth. Though they are both terrific types of dogs, both amazing with children and families and other animals (generally), they were bred to do totally different things and to react in totally different ways.

Pit bulls were largely (and sadly) bred to fight other dogs. So while dog reactivity would be bred into them, they needed to be "people passive"—that is, to be friendly and nonreactive toward humans. After all, a human hand needed to reach into the pit to stop the fighting. Rottweilers were originally bred to pull carts and protect livestock. They were bred to be wary of strangers—whether strange bears, wolves, or people. My dogs neither fought in pits nor protected livestock, and yet those cultivated instincts live on.

Somehow, this gives me hope for how we can cultivate our own instincts toward God. God gave us bodies and brains wired to notice and respond to the natural and spiritual world—whether we go to a church or a synagogue or a mosque, or whether we are raised in any faith or not. We can shrug off these spiritual instincts as silly—or we can embrace them and cultivate them in the same way early, responsible dog breeders did.

If we want to develop an instinct for seeking God and doing good, God gave us the tools—deep in our psyches but also in Scripture, in nature, in spiritual practices. The more we tap into these, the keener our senses become and the better our responses get.

Poet Gerard Manley Hopkins says, "The world is *charged* with the grandeur of God." When I read Hopkins, I think of the elephants and rabbits and birds who traveled up and away even before the tsunami's flood waters charged toward them. Whether they felt the earth shift through hoof, paw, or talon, or whether they smelled danger by putting snout to sky, the instincts animals share—and that humans can cultivate—are part of that grandeur.

7

FEAR

HOW TO PET A SNAKE

———◦———

I lay back, stretched next to my husband and kids across a rickety picnic table on the shores of Green Bay. Others all around us are doing just the same. We're campers at Door County, in Wisconsin's Peninsula State Park, all waiting for dusk to fall and for thousands of bats to emerge from the attic of a century-old cabin. The air around us bristles with excitement. The kids can't wait.

But me? I'm bristling with fear. Though my appreciation for bats has grown over the years, and though I can now happily watch them fly high above my house in the evenings and give thanks for the good mosquito-eating service they provide, I'm not sure if my lifelong fear of these leathery, fangy, flying beasts is really conquered. Here on this beautiful night, in beautiful woods, on a beautiful bay, I'm about to find out.

And I do as squeals of delight ring out all around me and the sky blackens with the wing-wooshes of a billion bats flying just above my head.

———

Reading a book like this one, you might assume that the author loves all creatures. You might picture the author preparing to snuggle when a friend offers to let her hold their slinky (and stinky) ferret. You may imagine the author cheering when a mouse scurries across the kitchen floor. You might even believe that, were the author to come mask-to-pointy-face with a barracuda while snorkeling, she'd thank God for the glimpse of this glory.

But if that author in question were me, you'd be very wrong.

Of course, I do love all creatures—in theory. I am not, however, a fan of all of them. And while I've loved animals my whole life, two animals have completely, irrationally terrified me for as long as I can remember: bats and snakes. Whether it's the stretched-leather wings or the long slow slither, or whether it's the possibility of one getting tangled in my hair or crawling up my leg, the very thought of bats and snakes sends shivers.

Of course, sharks and jellyfish scare me when I'm swimming in the ocean (in all fairness, though, so does seaweed). I get nervous seeing alligator warning signs in Florida, especially when my kids step too near a pond. But I don't recoil at pictures of sharks, jellyfish, or alligators, nor do I avoid looking at them behind enclosures. Were I to bumble into a lion while roaming the savanna, and were it to shake the trees with its growl and flash its bloodied teeth, I'm sure I'd be afraid. But somewhere, deep in my fantasies, I'm still convinced that my doggy-baby talk would lull the lion into passivity and allow me to snuggle up into its full mane.

As noted, neighborhood coyotes and foxes bring me great joy. Squirrels only scare me when they pop out of garbage cans (which actually happens fairly frequently). And like I said earlier, I am dangerously unafraid of all dogs. The ones I should be most nervous about—the hurt or scared ones tucking back into corners or under bushes—are the ones I'm most drawn to help. I've been bitten more times than I care to admit, but I'm still not afraid. I can't even *imagine* being afraid.

So while I realize plenty of animals pose actual danger to me, as a potentially delicious or threatening human, I haven't *felt* afraid at the thought of most of them. Except.

Bats and snakes both appear on Animal Planet's list of "Top 10 Animals That Scare Us the Most." (Coyotes are also on this list! What?). But still, my fear of these creatures has always been irrational. Blame it on the warning signs about "free-flying" fruit bats in the Australia House at Brookfield Zoo. Perhaps the warning sunk too deeply into my psyche, and I ended up so worried the entire time that one would get tangled in my hair that I couldn't even delight in the wombats.

And snakes? Shudder. Though the snakes in my Chicagoland neck of the woods are frequently unseen, mostly harmless, and totally beneficial, still—ugh. Wildlife biologists like Chris Anchor tell us that "snakes are nothing to be afraid of, particularly not in the Chicago region." He goes so far as to encourage us to feel "lucky" and to "enjoy watching" from a safe distance if we see one on a hike.

I'm running back to the car if that happens. But I appreciate his enthusiasm and assurance that I need *not* be afraid. In fact, his words remind me of my own statements when I'm eschewing the virtues of the most feared dogs.

I once listened to a man tell me exactly what it was about pit bulls that scared him. As I listened, I mentally rolled my eyes as I judged his ignorance and ridiculousness. *What a fool*, I thought as I prepared every counterargument I could to shut down his fear. But as I did so, something clicked in the back of my brain: *What about snakes?*

What *about* snakes? I wanted to yell back at the annoying voice in my head. But it was true. While I maintain that a fear of a *domestic* animal like a dog is indeed more ridiculous than of a *wild* animal like a freaking python—even one bred, born, and raised in captivity—I wondered how my own fears sounded to the ears of snake enthusiasts.

It hurts me to hear that people are afraid of my sweet, sweet dog. It enraged me when my mothering skills were questioned because we raised our babies with pit bulls and Rottweilers. Would it hurt herpetologists to hear my fears about their beloved snakes—to know I too wondered about the sanity of folks who kept snakes and *children* in the same home?

As it turns out, a little bit. Most people who love or study snakes, like dog enthusiasts, welcome a sensible fear. But they also like to point out that not all our fears are as founded as we think. That slippery little garter snake in my garden is *not*, apparently, going to kill me. Or even bite me. Nor will most snakes.

According to one Australian snake catcher, we know snakes are "happy" when they just skim along the ground with their necks as fat as their bodies and their tongues flicking in and out. Snakes get scared when surprised, and yet they are nice enough to give us fair warning with a raised head, fanned neck, and a solid hiss before going for the kill—er, the bite. This is just like a dog's handy warning growl. Other times snakes will offer the courtesy of a "dry bite." That is, they *could* do more damage but choose not to. It's almost endearing.

Not all snakes are as courteous. Pythons apparently don't do much to warn, probably because they don't have to. They aren't really afraid of us. They can, after all, kill and swallow prey five times bigger than their heads.

All this to say, I am still afraid of snakes. But I'm working on it. In fact, I've asked the snake-loving daughter of a good friend to tell me nice things about her snakes. I've even cooed at and *petted* one of her snakes—a giant, shedding yellow Burmese python. At any moment, the python could have cranked open its mouth and eaten me. And yet it didn't. Fear not, perhaps.

Years ago, a colleague casually mentioned that the Bible mentions fear more than "any other sin."

Sin? This was the first time I'd considered fear a sin. Obviously, classifying fear as sin is tricky. It is, after all, an important instinct. Fear of getting burned keeps us away from fire. Fear of dying of thirst keeps us seeking water. Fear of getting bit by—oh, say—a rattlesnake keeps us backing up when we hear a rattle in the desert. And of course, fear of the Lord is a thing to be admired.

And yet again and again, we read God telling us not to be afraid in the Scriptures. According to some sources, the commandment "do not fear" is given 365 times in the Bible. That's one "do not fear" for every day of the year! I have not counted myself, so I cannot confirm this is true. But certainly, we know that "do not fear" appears exponentially more times than other commands against sins we trouble ourselves with.

And if fear has any relationship to sin at all, it's probably not a sin in the vein of murder, oppressing others, or ignoring injustice. This is more about missing the mark or wandering away. So perhaps the Bible speaks against fear because being afraid can get in the way of doing what we're supposed to or going where we're supposed to. And so throughout the Scriptures, we hear God telling people to be not afraid. In Deuteronomy 31:8, we read, "The Lord himself goes before you and will be with you; he will never leave you nor forsake you. Do not be afraid; do not be discouraged" (NIV). In Joshua 1:9, God tells the people, "Do not be afraid; do not be discouraged, for the Lord your God will be with you wherever you go" (NIV).

The angels are always telling people to "fear not" (think Mary, Joseph, the poor shepherds, and the women who came to tend to Jesus's body). Jesus tells us not to worry and to "take heart" (John 16:33 NIV). Both are clear variations of "do not fear."

And Paul—who, for all his faults, was quite brave and survived shipwreck snake attacks!—both was told by God not to be afraid and reminds the Philippians not to be anxious about anything (Philippians 4:6–7). Peter tells us not only to *not* be afraid but to "cast all [our] anxiety" on God because God cares (1 Peter 5:7).

But no one—not one other person—in all of Scripture talks about "do not fear[ing]" quite the way Isaiah does. Saint Peter agrees with me on this, since when Peter tells us not to fear, he quotes Isaiah, the Eloquent Fear Master. Consider these passages:

Do not fear, for I am with you,
do not be afraid, for I am your God;

I will strengthen you, I will help you,
 I will uphold you with my victorious
  right hand. (Isaiah 41:10)

Do not fear, you worm Jacob,
 you insect Israel!
I will help you, says the Lord;
 your Redeemer is the Holy One of Israel.
  (Isaiah 41:14)

And in case you want to know why the little worm doesn't need to be afraid, the writer, in the voice of God, clarifies *how* God will help:

Now, I will make of you a threshing sledge,
 sharp, new, and having teeth;
you shall thresh the mountains and crush
 them,
  and you shall make the hills like chaff.
You shall winnow them and the wind shall
 carry them away,
  and the tempest shall scatter them.
  (Isaiah 41:15–16)

Now, I'm something of a pacifist. War language doesn't normally move me. But when it's as crafted as masterfully as Isaiah writes, look out. I read these words and think, *I can do anything with the God who makes us threshing sledges!*

But this passage isn't even Isaiah at his best. No, God gives Isaiah such a powerful picture of God's presence that we can give up fear for good. Well, almost. Isaiah 43—one of my favorite passages in all of Scripture—begins this way:

> *But now, this is what the Lord says—*
> *he who created you, Jacob,*
> *he who formed you, Israel:*
> *"Do not fear, for I have redeemed you;*
> *I have summoned you by name; you are*
> *mine." (Isaiah 43:1 NIV)*

As if being redeemed, summoned by name, and belonging to the Lord of the Universe weren't enough reason not to fear, God gets specific. God follows the classic writing advice of show, don't tell:

> *When you pass through the waters,*
> *I will be with you;*
> *and when you pass through the rivers,*
> *they will not sweep over you.*
> *When you walk through the fire,*
> *you will not be burned;*
> *the flames will not set you ablaze.*

For I am the Lord your God,
   the Holy One of Israel, your Savior.
   (Isaiah 43:2–3 NIV)

And with that, the "do not fear" mic drops.

This last passage is a metaphor, of course. We all
know that many God-fearing people have drowned.
Too many saints burned to death—many at the stake,
at the hands of "God-fearing" people! But this metaphor does a couple things for us. One, while the
images are specific, the message is general—and clear.
The message is not that no one will ever die in fire or
water. Instead, it's that God is with us. Not only is
God *with* us, but God *goes* with us. God enters those
raging rivers. God steps into the roaring fires. And
that is why we don't have to be afraid. Rivers
and fires can do their best to terrify us—to stop us
from moving forward and pressing on. But God's presence with us means we don't need to be afraid. Those
fires and rivers can do their best to kill, to maim, to
destroy, and to deter. But God is not thwarted by
the power of creation. And we shouldn't be either.

The second thing this metaphor does is offer us the
opportunity to rewrite. To personalize and shape and
apply it to our context. As far as I'm concerned, we
might just as well imagine God saying to us, "When

you see that slither and hear that rattle, the bite will not sink deep, the venom will not paralyze you! For when you step into the path of that snake, I am with you! I am the Lord your God, the creator and master of snakes."

Lest you think this is silly, God *does* tell Job he didn't need to fear the wild animals (Job 5:22). This doesn't mean that no snake will ever again bite anyone (or slowly constrict them—Lord have mercy). But it means that God goes with us. That God *is* with us. And that the snake cannot deter God. And so neither should it deter us.

Because of course life is scary. Speaking opinions is scary. Raising kids is scary. Stepping into our calling is scary. We can't go a day without something to terrify us. But when we give into fear, we lose out on the life we are meant to live and on the things we are called to do.

Fear may not be a sin. But no matter what you call it—sin, natural emotion, instinctual threat alert—fear can stop us from doing God's will. It can prevent us from speaking up or out, and it can deter us from taking that important next step or facing a hard situation. You see the problem.

God calls us into all sorts of fires, all sorts of raging rivers. God calls us to live among bats and snakes. Sometimes these are metaphors, sometimes they are quite literal. Especially when God calls us to face those fears.

───────────

In that Wisconsin dusk, as the tiny brown bats flapped their leathery wings what seemed like just centimeters from my face, I joined in on the chorus of delighted squeals. My kids and I clapped as they passed. We couldn't stop smiling after the millionth (or so it seemed) bat flapped over us toward its twilight meal in the woods beyond.

As I sat up to watch them disappear into the woods, I couldn't imagine that I was ever afraid of these magnificent creatures. And yet I had been— proudly—until one night in college, when my cute neighbor pointed them out flying above us in the dusky sky. Rather than have a heart attack right in front of him, I played it cool and looked up. My breath caught, but not out of fear. Instead, I was mesmerized watching those black shadows dip and dash against an inky sky in a dusk ballet—a ballet that eats mosquitos.

Suddenly, my fears seemed so ridiculous. These animals were *not* scary; they were dazzling. And they opened up a whole new world to me—the night sky. Honestly, I'd spent very little time looking up at twilight, waiting instead for the deep dark before I looked up at starry skies. But in observing the bats, I saw birds taking last-light flights. I saw tree branches—bare or leaf-fluffed—swaying. To this day, twilight is the time I hear most clearly the whisper of the Spirit.

Facing my fear of bats had done this. It had allowed me to answer an invitation to hear from God. I recognized this again as we watched the pure glory of a sky darken with flapping bats. I wish I could say my fear of snakes has gone the way of bats. But alas, I'm still pretty nervous around them. Yet I'm confident that an appreciation of snakes will open up new worlds of wonder—either that or kill me (just kidding!). Maybe someday, a growing curiosity about snakes will show me many things about the God who thought they were a most excellent idea.

8

CREATIVE ABUNDANCE

WHY THE OCTOPUS CHANGES COLOR

I shrugged. "Looks like a big red maple leaf," I said.

Never mind that we were wading in Pacific Ocean waters off of a San Diego beach—hardly a spot known for its huge maples. And never mind that this was July, when even the most monstrous maples hold tight to their green and silvery leaves, their red hues months away.

And so my son and his cousin kept jumping over and diving into the waves, never minding the "maple leaf" floating around their torsos—until it brushed up against them and stung.

They were fine. I mean, after the lifeguard showed us how to treat the sting (not with urine, by the way!) and told us to watch for a serious reaction. The cousins came away with a great story about being attacked by a giant red jellyfish.

"Maple leaf . . ." they repeated throughout the trip, rolling their eyes at my ridiculous blunder. I came away with guilt over my child-harming stupidity and wonderment over *why* I had failed to ask the question I have asked nearly every other time I've entered a body of water: What *else* swims here?

I often read up on the local underwater creatures before we travel. I certainly pay attention to the warning signs. Unless we're talking about sea snakes, it's not that I'm afraid of sea creatures. I just like to know what might be brushing up against my leg or what I might open my eyes and see. But this trip? I had spent little to no time considering what swam along in the depths and shallows of Southern California's Pacific waters. I took for granted that the sea lions were all happily barking on rocks in La Jolla and assumed any wayward sharks would take out a surfer long before they got to us waders and wave-hoppers. Jellyfish had not even entered my mind. Wasn't it too cold for them? Perhaps it was too cold for the clear, round jellies I was accustomed to in the Gulf of Mexico, but apparently not this hardy red variety.

But my misstep, and our maple-leafy jellyfish friend, did more than just fill me with shame and regret. They reminded me of the vast mysteries our deep lakes, seas, and oceans hold. It seems the waters, unlike any other place, astound us with new wonders and discoveries with every visit. And not just with the things that we can see or that surprise us. After all, the waters teem with creatures that for most of human civilization have gone unnoted. If they didn't rise to the surface or allow themselves to be caught in a net, no one knew they were there.

And even when we suspected or imagined creatures were there—think sea monsters or mermaids—we got this very wrong. Yet we got it wrong for good reason. Our suspicions about unbelievable creatures of the deep were correct. We were right to imagine these fantastical things. Because these creatures have been there all along, often with even weirder and wilder fan-tailed shapes or siren-singing sounds than we could have ever dreamed up. And they've been there for millions and billions of years—out of sight, if not out of mind. Since the dawn of time, sea creatures have existed for the benefit of our imaginations, our ecosystem, and for God alone. And they have spoken so eloquently to God's absolutely decadent abundance and creativity.

The first time I scrolled through Neal Agarwal's virtual deep-sea dive called "The Deep Sea," my breath caught. The second time, I couldn't stop smiling. Each time after that, my eyes widened, and my eyebrows raised as I waited to see if it was any less astounding. It never was. Even now, no matter how many times I do it, it never is. How could we not be astounded by traveling down 532 meters, the depth of an emperor penguin's dive, or by staring into the "midnight depths" with the bioluminescent goblin sharks who have swum the darkness for 125 million years? How could we not be astounded by technology that causes our hearts to race as we sink deeper and deeper through jet-blackness until at last a sea pig appears? By the fact that we haven't even reached the deepest depths?

At 6,446 meters deep, a blurb reminds us, "The deep sea can be a lonely place." Indeed. Yet the psalmist reminds us that God is there:

Where can I go from your Spirit?
 Where can I flee from your presence?
If I go up to the heavens, you are there;
 if I make my bed in the depths, you are
 there. (Psalm 139:7–8 NIV)

And indeed, signs of God's presence and creativity are all over the deep sea. Along the way down to the depths, we pass places where fewer people have been than have landed on the moon. We sink deeper than the heights of Mount Everest, and we learn of two men, Jacques Piccard and Don Walsh, who braved terrifying pressure and lack of oxygen to reach Challenger Deep, the deepest point of the ocean. Even as they dived nearly eleven thousand meters, they could still see life out the windows. "Life can survive unimaginable environments," Agarwal writes.

Though Agarwal describes himself as a "developer with a passion for creative coding" who loves "pushing the limits of the web and creating fun digital experiences," his deep-sea "experience" pushes more than the limits of the internet. As we scroll down, down, down—past the limits of what human beings can survive—and take in the creatures who live in these dark depths, it pushes the limits of both our imagination and our theology.

Because people of faith *do* have a theology when it comes to humans and animals. Whether it's a theology we've given much thought to or not, we've got one. Except for the most committed animal rights activists among us—I am interested in animal welfare, not necessarily animal rights, and there is a difference—I'd guess that most Christians still take seriously Genesis 1's mandate to care for and steward the creatures of the land and sea, even if we disagree about what that looks like (some of us believe animals are fine to eat and ride, for instance, while others disagree).

Yet we run into trouble when we start thinking about the deepest of sea creatures. After all, what care can we take for the hadal amphipod, who lives its life in the cold and dark and under pressure that would kill us humans? How can we steward its future?

Most caretakers understand, at least partially, those in their care. Kings and queens *know* their realm. Shepherds know their flock. They understand those they rule over and care for. It is this way for us with most animals. I may *fear* snakes—but I understand them (or I'm learning to). Their presence and their life make sense to me. But the lonely pink cusk eel at 8,300 meters deep? Why? What on earth (or in the sea) is that thing *for*?

Surely scientists can tell me their purpose—the role they play in the marine ecosystem. Surely the world and the oceans would be worse off without them. But somehow, I believe they exist simply, purely, for the glory of God. God created this world because God so loved it; that means God loves people and plants and weird creatures of the deep. God's creativity and God's love are so abundant that the wild creatures of this world are likewise abundant. It doesn't matter if another human or a piece of technology ever sees these creatures. God knows they are there. And that is enough.

Especially since these creatures love their Creator right back.

I have long found it endearing that the psalmist chose to include the sea monsters in the litany of created things that praise the Lord. (Different translations call these sea creatures by different names. The King James Version calls them "dragons." What trouble this must make for biblical literalists!) After all, sea monsters are fearsome things—and not just to sailors who worried about floating about with these monsters.

In ancient Jewish folklore, the seas also contained sea *demons*—the Leviathan and Rabab. In the Scriptures, more times than not, when the Hebrew word *tannin* is used for sea monsters, we're talking about evil beings out to bring chaos and destruction. Creatures that God will defeat.

Throughout the ancient world, the Leviathan wreaked havoc on the seas. They caused the water to boil. They ate one whale each day (according to one midrash, Jonah's big fish only narrowly escaped the Leviathan's jaws—what an interesting twist *that* would have been to an already twisted tale!). These were creatures that struck fear into the hearts of sailors—and even the land-dwellers who never ever stuck a toe in the water.

Yet in Psalm 148:7, we read, "Praise the Lord from the earth, you sea monsters and all deeps . . ."—right alongside princes and fruit trees and "creeping things" in the psalmists' *Who's Who* of who needs to praise God. It's spectacular.

But also, as we think about it—it's not *that* far-fetched. We can imagine why the ancients were so fascinated with creatures of the deep. It's no wonder stories of mermaids and sirens took hold. Though it's tempting to roll our eyes at the ancient sailors who fretted about the huge monsters swimming under their crafts, it's no wonder they did!

And it wasn't just *ancient* sailors who did this. Just a few centuries ago, my seafaring Swedish ancestors told tales of the fearsome Kraken—a sea monster described by Swedish author Jacob Wallenberg in 1781 as "not that huge" and "no larger than our Öland is wide."

For those not familiar with "our Öland"—say, if your grandmother didn't hail from the island as mine did—allow me to explain. Öland is indeed not very wide. Not even ten miles at its widest spot. But still, Wallenberg is estimating that the crabby Kraken is about ten miles wide! No wonder these seafarers often confused this creature with an island and believed its crabby legs kickstarted whirlpools.

Plenty of humans still believe in creatures of the deep (hello, Loch Ness monster!). Or at least, we enjoy imagining they are there. It's no wonder. There is something about the mysteries of water—of the deep, of its unattainability—that stirs our imaginations unlike anything else, except perhaps space.

I've wondered if it did the same for God.

———

Öland sits off the coast of southeast Sweden, between the Kalmar Strait to the west and the brackish waters of the Baltic Sea to the east. The island is pure magic. Not simply because you can practically see the cone-hatted *tomte* (think Swedish elves) rushing through the wildflowers and ducking behind rocks on the alvar, but because of the *water*. The water surrounding Öland has a spirit like none other I've ever been around or in.

The Kalmar Strait offers long stretches of shallow sea and welcomes waders into its clear, bracing water. The beaches along western Öland are among the most beautiful I've ever visited. Granted, I am biased; it's my ancestral home. To be fair, my grandmother spoke frequently of the beauty of the island, but I don't remember hearing much about the water. Apparently poor farmers' daughters in the early 1900s didn't spend much time at the beach. Still, one can hardly grow up on a Swedish island and *not* be shaped by water. Indeed, my grandmother fearlessly crossed the Atlantic alone at sixteen. Once arriving in America, she stopped short of her intended destination—arid Denver—to make her new life in Chicago, just blocks from Lake Michigan.

Back in Sweden for a family trip, as we stood on the land my grandmother and her family once farmed, we could smell the sea air from the mighty Baltic lapping at the shore up the road. Suddenly my grandmother's claims of hearing World War I cannons firing across the sea in Poland didn't seem so implausible. Indeed, that mighty body of water that laps at the shores of Sweden, Denmark, Germany, Poland, Finland, Estonia, Lithuania, and Russia has carried sound and culture and stories across its body for eons.

When we drove east and I stood before the Baltic's wild waters, in a field where cows mooed and milled, my own mind reeled with the sounds, culture, and stories that had been carried across those waters. As we headed north and I stood in a Baltic harbor full of fishing trawlers, my mind dived deeper, and I wondered about the life that lived *beneath* those waters.

The fish case inside and menu board outside the harbor fish market told us that the waters teemed with prawns and haddock, lobsters and crawfish, oysters and the herring that have made themselves a staple of Swedish cuisine—even among those who emigrated from these shores.

From the surface of the water, one might imagine only the blandest sea life would survive the frigid, barely saline waters. But of course, that is not the case. Google tells me sharks swim those waters. The Smithsonian shows me that barnacle-covered crabs; fuzzy, floppy corals; flat flounder; bright-white and orange mollusks; and frog-like snail fish swim above the often-frozen seabed.

For the nearly eight thousand years that people have inhabited Öland, many of these creatures were unknown. The island's inhabitants knew what they caught—and what swam to the surface. Yet clearly people have always sensed the creativity and abundance of what exists far beneath the waters. While sea creatures may give us few clues to and glimpses of their existence, when they come to the surface, they surprise us.

People rightly wonder about the first humans to cook and crack open a lobster or crawfish. Who first saw the hard shell and grabby claws and thought,

"Yum!"? Obviously, a hungry person. But also, probably someone who understood that the Creator was just that creatively abundant—to fill the seas with mysterious creatures that might also happen to be delicious.

The seas continue to prove that God's creativity knows no limits. In fact, while it may seem ridiculous to some for the ancients and not-so-ancients to have dreamed up sea dragons and mermaids when they were staring into the wide oceans or swift rivers or murky Scottish lochs, such creatures are no more fantastical than what *God* dreamed up. After all, God first filled those seas with plants and creatures, ready to adapt and evolve, knowing it would be billions of years before anyone or anything on land would encounter or appreciate them. (My land-centrism is obviously showing here. Clearly, the reverse is also true!) This is, after all, the God who made octopuses that change color with their dreams and who made axolotls so cute we could snuggle them.

No imaginary creature can come close to the creativity of our God. And yet any time we try to come up with one, we simply reflect that impulse.

———

Two summers ago, as I stood in the bone-chilling shallows of the Kalmar Strait while family members and summer-loving Swedes jumped off a pier, I fought off feelings of guilt for having returned to this island with such American excess. After a day of traveling to my family's former farmland, and after standing before their baptismal and burial spots, we had knocked on a stranger's door to see the inside of the tiny (but so, so adorable) cottage that once housed my grandmother's family of eight. And then my family had waded in the waters of the Kalmar Strait in front of our rented condo just off the gorgeous beach. I thought of what these waters meant to my family—and how they shaped us.

I looked across the strait toward mainland Sweden. When my grandmother emigrated nearly one hundred years prior, she'd have taken a ferry across these waters to reach Kalmar, then taken a train to Gothenburg, where she would have boarded yet another ship and crossed the North Sea, and then the Atlantic.

Though these great bodies of water separated her from her family for decades, crossing them also granted her opportunities. To lose herself and to gain. Looking across those waters, her imagination must have stirred right alongside her fear. Even as she must have worried what was ahead, so too did she wonder. And that's what the sea does for us. That's what I believe God *wants* the waters to do for us: humble us, pacify us, terrify us, and inspire us.

After all, when we first meet the Spirit in the Scriptures, she is hovering, a wind above the waters, inspiring what's created above and beneath her. A few "days" later, according to Genesis 1:20–21, "God said, 'Let the waters bring forth swarms of living creatures. . . .' So God created the great sea monsters and every living creature that moves, of every kind, with which the waters swarm. . . . And God saw that it was good."

Perhaps this is why even when the ancients imagined the sea creatures as terrifying, they could still imagine them as praising God. After all, it was our creative God who whispered them into existence and declared them good.

9

CURIOSITY

WHAT KILLS THE CAT MAKES US LOVE IT

———◉———

Traffic ahead slows, then stops. Although this is a major road—six lanes at this point—that cuts through crowded suburban strip malls and shopping centers, past restaurants and office complexes, no one honks. (Well, not the drivers.) We all just stop. Some put their cars in park. Those of us close enough to see what's happening smile as the geese hop off the curb and waddle across the lanes, fuzzy babies and lanky teenagers in tow.

It's just another Canada goose traffic jam. And while it's frustrating for those of us who have some place to get to (and don't we always?), nothing restores my faith in the decency of humanity more than dozens of cars all stopping to save the lives of pesky creatures. And these geese *are* pesky—and often mean!

Once upon a time, the flying Vs across Chicago-land heralded colder weather as the migratory Canada geese made their way from the far north (Thunder Bay, Ontario, was often the town I heard) to warmer climes. Back then, we'd look up at their honking and wave as they flew over. We'd wonder how they knew to form the V, we'd worry if they were getting tired, and we'd hope they had safe travels. Well, at least, I would. Back then, they were magical and mystical, creatures of pure curiosity you'd only see wandering on land if you were lucky.

Today, geese are Chicagoland staples. These Canada geese seek and find their warmer climes right here in the Midwest. Although Chicago certainly is warmer than Thunder Bay, Ontario, these magnificent birds *could* fly hundreds more miles to warmer places. But they choose to stay in a place where they flap across ice and poke their beaks through snow. Kentucky, probably just a few days' flight at most, is *much* warmer in the winter. Odd if you ask me—or, as it turns out, researchers from the University of Illinois.

Certainly, the researchers were prompted by the countless Chicagoans who have been wondering why geese have taken up residence in such abundance and why they are now year-round mainstays. They swarm our parks, ball fields, and parking lots. They linger at schools, offices, golf courses, and churches—anywhere green space or a pond can be found. They worry airline pilots and stop traffic on busy roads. Office complexes employ territorial swans or border-collie wranglers, and schools set fake coyotes in fields to try to scare away the birds and minimize the poop.

So of course, we wonder why. Most of us had guessed—correctly—that climate change, heated ponds, and decreased predators (despite that strong coyote comeback) were among the reasons. Dr. Michael Ward, an associate professor in the Department of Natural Resources and Environmental Sciences at the University of Illinois at Urbana-Champaign, wanted to know for sure, so he and his team fitted geese with tracking devices and began studying their migration patterns.

What they found was shocking—at least to me. Geese stay in Chicago in part because it is safe. Specifically, here in these parts, they are safe from gunfire. Now Chicago is one of the great (if not greatest) cities on the planet, but "safe" is not often a word used to describe it. Gun violence in this beautiful, world-class city town is among the highest in the country—for humans. But not toward geese. Hunting doesn't happen.

Ward and his team discovered that since they don't have to fly off from hunters, geese conserve energy. Urban areas don't provide the same amount of corn to pick through as farmland does, obviously, but conserving energy is of higher value. And this pays off: twice as many geese survive their winter in Chicago as do those that fly to warmer spots.

———

Curiosity may kill the cat. But it's curiosity (theirs and ours) that endears cats, dogs, geckos, and every living thing to us. Although we love animals because they are cute, funny, helpful, and comforting—and because at least some of them love us back so well—it's often their *oddness* and curiousness that first draws us to them.

Curiosity about fire and food brought the first wolves creeping up to early human campfires. Curiosity caused the first humans to straddle a horse and take that first wild ride off into the sunset. Curiosity marches us off into woods with binoculars or swims us out into seas with snorkels. Curiosity fuels visits to zoos and aquariums and sparks research at universities (as well as at good zoos and aquariums!).

Our ability to wonder about animals is endless. We could watch our own pets or neighborhood animals and *never* run out of questions. And as we've already explored, there's a whole giant planet filled with creatures that never fail to compel.

Of course, no matter how many questions we ask or how much research into animal behavior or physiology is done, animals remain a mystery. We can now train dogs to settle enough to get an MRI, and we can tag, trace, and observe animal patterns and behaviors. We can spend millions of dollars and endless hours of brainpower to fuel research to better understand animals every year. Still, as with everything, it seems the more we know, the more questions we have.

Just as a scent leads a hound over asphalt and wood chips, through woods and down creek beds, so our curiosity about our animal friends leads us down trails and paths of wonderment. And this is a good, good thing.

Our Creator made this world *interesting*. God set odd behaviors and quirks into creatures—humans not least among them!—not to trick or confound us but to fascinate us, to captivate us, and to get us in the habit of asking, of wondering, of discovering. It seems God did this to help us become very comfortable in the mystery of creation and its Creator.

═══════

Two days after writing about the "imaginary" Leviathan in the previous chapter, I hit a snag about God. This happens every so often. Though I *believe* in God, I also doubt God. Routinely. Just when I think I've got it, just when I think my faith is settled and sure(ish), something happens to trip me up. Now some will claim that doubt is the result of spiritual warfare, the work of the evil one. I am, after all, knee-deep in seminary. I work at a church and feel called deeper and deeper into ministry all the time. I write about God and faith. Some might suggest I'm a prime target for the hooks and horns of the local demons.

And indeed, I'm a believer in the spiritual realm. I believe in ghosts. I believe in the presence of angels and demons—and that they busy themselves defending us or tripping us up, respectively. I've sensed it. I've felt it. I've known it.

Yet when doubt strikes—when I find myself asking the big *why*s and *how*s about God—I don't ever sense evil at work. In fact, I feel quite the opposite:

I believe it's pure Holy Spirit, which I admit is odd for a doubter to believe. But thus far, my forty-plus years of big doubts and bigger questions have not yet turned me away from God—at least, not ultimately. They've only brought me nearer.

For instance, just two days after writing about the Leviathan and how people *imagined* it—and how that made us more like our imaginative, creative God—I read these words from God in Job 40 and 41: "Look at Behemoth, which I made just as I made you" (Job 40:15). Now Behemoth, like the Leviathan, is a creature of *legend*. While we just talked about how good and imaginative God is, it seems a little strange for God to say God *made* this make-believe being. It would be no different than God saying, "Look at Bigfoot, which I made just as I made you." I hope I'm not the only one who finds this troubling!

So naturally, as I read this line, I find myself asking God, *When exactly did you create the imaginary Behemoth?* Then I hold on to this question as I read on to the next chapter. Now God asks Job in Job 41:1, "Can you draw out Leviathan with a fishhook, or press down its tongue with a cord?"

No he can't, God. And neither can you! I want to say. Because I know God is okay with this. And I know—from decades of blasting God with my doubts while reading the Bible—that God will give it right back. And indeed, I feel my mind going toward the "think different" space to which the Spirit always leads me in my doubts.

As I think differently, I come up with the following: One, the chapter is a reminder to Job about who Job is (a human, limited in power and ability) and who God is (unlimited in power and ability). While Job is not a fun book by a long stretch, God gets seriously *silly* in the insistence that God alone is all-powerful. Consider God's question in Job 41:5: "Will you play with [the Leviathan] as with a bird, or will you put it on leash for your girls?"

This is a fantastic image. Even Job—in his terrible, terrible state—must have cracked a smile. And this silliness leads us to something else that is going on. God is *entering* into Job's (presently very troubled) world. What's important here isn't whether the Leviathan or Behemoth are real or not. What matters is that *Job* believes in the Leviathan and Behemoth. In fact, they are probably the most terrifying creatures people of Job's day can imagine. Real or not, they symbolize the mightiest creatures alive.

So God isn't contesting the reality of these creatures but simply asserting God's power. Whereas these creatures terrify Job, God could throw a leash on the Leviathan and offer them to our daughters as a pet. This is a picture of every parent singing silly songs to the monsters under the bed and bringing them into the game. *We* know no monsters lurk in the closets; it's what our kids believe that matters. So we show them we are more powerful than the monsters.

This still doesn't explain why God said God *made* them. But this could be the result of a few other things. First, God created our imaginations. Depending on our view of God's sovereignty (and for all my doubts, I have a pretty high view), this means God makes what we create. At the very least, God is the God of our creative minds and imaginations. As someone who writes fiction for children and creates characters all the time, I find it moving to contemplate that God is God of the characters I create.

And speaking of creating characters and writing fiction, some biblical scholars believe that the book of Job is a work of fiction. It's not hard to imagine why. In Job, we see God taking Satan up on a challenge—a wager, of sorts, over Job's faithfulness. That should be enough to make us disbelieve the book. Also, the conversations with Job's friends are so detailed that it's hard to imagine who was taking dictation.

If this were true—if the book *were* created as a work of fiction to help us understand why there is good and evil in the world—we could understand why the human authors would have had God saying these words about creating make-believe creatures.

It's like Neil Gaiman's paraphrase of G. K. Chesterton in the epigraph to *Coraline*: "Fairy tales are more than true; not because they tell us dragons exist, but because they tell us dragons can be beaten."

Of course, God could have been saying the same thing. I am about as far from a scholar on the book of Job as I am from being an astronaut. But even if it *were* fiction, it's still *true*. As is so much fiction! So even if these conversations were made up, these words from God—the famous assurance of who "laid the foundations of the earth"—are right as rain. And in these questions God asks Job, God leads us to wonder, to imagine, to go deep into who God is.

And while this passage is still curious, I realize two things: One, we will never fully know why God said this. And that's okay, because two, I like a God who would offer a little girl the Leviathan on a leash.

———

"First somewhat substantial snow of the season today," historian and author Kristin Du Mez tweeted, along with a photograph of a circle of dog tracks in the snow. "And this is what our dog thought of that." It's funny. Those of us who know dogs *know* what her dog thought. Not a fan. Peed quickly and hurried inside.

But just two days after her tweet, I noted curious tracks in our own freshly fallen snow. From the "fingers," I could tell they were raccoon tracks—although the sleety snow had left them splayed and distorted, with an otherworldly quality. But freakier than the tracks themselves was the pattern. They started at my car door and looped all through the back of our driveway, under the basketball hoop, toward the fence gate, and then back toward the garbage cans. No straight lines. No direct paths.

I smiled at the paw-stamped loops and waves across my icy driveway. Perhaps the raccoon was chasing a mouse (heroically keeping it from entering our house?), but the pattern looked like the feet of a creature having *fun*. Like it was playing in the slush. Standing at my back gate, arms full of flattened cardboard boxes and hoping the raccoon was not waiting for me by the recycling bin, I realized I would never know just what that raccoon was up to. Yet it was fun to wonder about and imagine, if only for a quick trip to the bins.

The same could be said for our dogs. Of course, we don't ever really know what our dogs "think" of something. We can guess. We can surmise. We can study and wonder and befriend and love. But we won't know until the blessed day when we can fully communicate.

And we have to be okay with this. We may be totally wrong about our insights into animals. The beauty of science is that it keeps surmising, changing, and adapting. And it keeps telling us more things we can be curious about, both helping us understand the world better and revealing more things we didn't know we didn't know. In the meantime, our place is within the mysteries of this creation and its Creator. I, for one, am good with that.

10

LIMINAL PLACES

WHERE THE CROWS LEAD

───────◉───────

I paused, my hand on the door handle, and prayed my dog would not notice. Though normally she didn't care about birds, catching sight of a red-tailed hawk perched on our deck rail might be just the thing to set her—and the hawk—off. So I crept backward and tried to distract her with food in her bowl, all the while keeping my eye on the brown-feathered bit of majesty just four feet away on the other side of the glass.

Successfully sidetracking our dog with a treat, I tiptoed back to the door. As I approached, the hawk turned toward me. Our eyes met. The whole universe narrowed into the magic of this moment and place. Then the hawk turned back toward the patch of dry grass and pile of twigs that we'd neglected to bag up. Its eyes steadied and its back straightened. Then it spread its wings, sprang, and snagged from the pile of twigs a mouse—*the* mouse, I imagined, that just the other day had startled me when I walked through the gate.

I smiled. Though hawks have not traditionally been viewed as signs of the Holy Spirit's presence, my local birds of prey have always been enough to spark in me reminders of God as eagle. And here, as this beautiful hawk snagged the mouse that had startled me, I felt the Spirit reminding me, "I'm here. I got this." My shoulders relaxed as another (non-mouse-related) anxiety eased.

Some people adopt animals or birds or other things in the world as spiritual or religious emblems of sorts—as reminders of God's presence. Some experience dragonflies or butterflies as visitors from God. I know some people who learn to see smiles on the faces of strangers as reminders of the goodness in the world. Alice Walker famously wrote of the color purple's ability to remind us of God. Others wear crosses, use rosaries, place statues in gardens. Jesus told us to remember him when we eat bread and drink wine together, which is as lovely a reminder as I can imagine. Indeed, throughout Scripture, we read of God calling God's people to *remember* in the sacred moments, in the everyday, and in everything in between. And God calls us to remember not only what God has done but that God is present.

Though there are many signs and symbols of God in this world, animals are among the most intimate and immediate. Because of the important role animals play in Scripture—pointing us back and up and *through* to God—they have always been portals and signposts for the liminal places where God is near.

═══════

My parents tell the story of the first time they took me to Disney World. I was two (Disney World, for what it's worth, was only four). While they excitedly pointed out Mickey and Minnie, Pluto and Goofy, Chip 'n' Dale, these costumed characters held none of my interest—and at times, all of my fear, as I indicated in the introduction. Instead, my parents will tell you, after spending all that money to fly me down to the "Happiest Place on Earth," I delighted in the chipmunks—the real kind—who darted into bushes with dropped pieces of popcorn.

Though I think of this story whenever I see a chipmunk—whether in Disney World, in the woods, or in my dorm room, as once happened—I had never attached any significance to it other than that I was a weird, animal-loving little girl (and now a weird, animal-loving grown woman). That is, until I was at Disney*land* several years ago. As we walked through the park, taking in all the magic and fun of the place, I spotted a gas station sign above the magical tree line. This wasn't a gas station sign for a Disney gas station. This was a sign for a station outside the park. In the real world.

Like the snap of a hypnotist's fingers, the spell of Disney was broken for me. With that sign, I was reminded that this wonderful world Disney had created for me was *not* all there was. Other life still happened, where real cars, taking real people to real jobs, still needed gas on the other side of the gates.

Now hear me: no matter how much I appreciate the creative genius of Walt Disney, I'm not comparing him to God. And I'm not saying Disneyland is earth and suburban Anaheim is heaven! But I *am* saying that we are parts of two worlds, if you will.

As people of faith, we believe in both our physical world and a spiritual one. (Disney is sort of a play physical one as opposed to the real physical one.) Since the dawn of humanity, spiritually inclined people have noted the times when and places where these worlds intersect or overlap—or at least allow us to peer from one into the other. The characters of the Old Testament told others about their encounters with God with clarity. The prophets decreed their experiences. And the mystics wrote of their interactions with the divine or spiritual world.

Certain faith traditions canonize saints based on their good deeds, miracles, and sightings that bleed between worlds. And of course, ghost stories exist because we so deeply want to believe that these worlds are never all that separate.

And indeed, I do believe this. I believe not only in two (perhaps more!) worlds. I also believe that these words enmesh and intersect in thin, or liminal, spaces.

A liminal space is simply an in-between space: the space between experience and opportunity, a border between nations, the summer between graduation and convocation, a space between any two things, really. A thin place *is* a liminal space, but a very specific one.

According to Eric Weiner, thin places "are locales where the distance between heaven and earth collapses and we're able to catch glimpses of the divine, or the transcendent or, as I like to think of it, the Infinite Whatever." Thin places can be anywhere. Because of the Celtic roots of thin place theology, we might imagine them on the misty green banks of Irish shores or perhaps in the holiest of spaces. However, according to Weiner, what matters more than

their location or the fact that they can happen anywhere is that they can happen any*when*. They are, he
writes, places where "time bursts its banks." (Sit with
that masterful image a moment.)

And indeed, thin places are often (and perhaps
always) ecstatic—meaning not necessarily happy
but thrilling. The presence of the divine rushes at
us, drenches us with the holy of the place and the
moment and the goodness of God in this world. In
these times, we not only "see" (or feel, taste, smell,
or hear) God, but we glimpse the *other*, better world
out there. When we step into thin places, we get to
see the world that exists now—both the physical and
the spiritual—but also, if we believe it, the world that
will one day exist: the new heaven and the new earth,
where all things are restored, made right.

But signs of the restored world are all around
us. We see it in the goodness and beauty of this world.
We see it in kindness and sacrificial and neighborly
love of friends and enemies alike. We see it when
we treat others and creation with dignity. We see it
in the miracles that still happen. We see it whenever
the then and the now, whenever the spiritual and
physical, touch. When Jesus talked about the kingdom of heaven or the kingdom of God (which exists
in the here and now), I imagine he meant exactly
these sorts of thin places.

And animals often take us to these thin places. Like their human counterparts, these saints of feather and fang that we love so much can point us not only to our Creator but to signs of God's presence and goodness all around. These animal saints also remind us that the world is full of thin places. If we notice animals—and chase them—they can point us to the thin places even in the midst of our "thick" ones. That's what those chipmunks were doing for me at Disney.

——

Of course, talking about saintly animals pointing us to places where we can see and feel God makes some Christians nervous. While we may talk about lions and lambs and love stories about big fish and manger-side donkeys, Christianity is hardly an animal-centric religion. Certainly intentionally so. Church fathers fought, blood and sweat, tooth and nail, to proclaim our somehow triune God, to differentiate their faith from the faith of our Jewish brothers and sisters, and to distance it from the faith of those polytheistic pagans. The *last* thing anyone needed was to bring *animals* into the mix. Certainly not the way the Egyptians did, worshipping dogs for their hunting and protecting acumen and of course cats for the good luck they brought and their magical abilities.

Today, invoking animals in any kind of spiritual manner evokes images of, well, *spirit* animals. Like so many things, white people have appropriated and often thus made an offensive mockery of the spiritual helpers, which are often animals, of many Indigenous communities. On the other hand, some Christians can't understand the importance of these spiritual helpers, and the idea of invoking animals as spirit guides makes them uncomfortable.

To them, I claim general revelation—the idea that *everything in nature* points to God. "The earth is the Lord's and *everything* in it," we read in Psalm 24:1, "the world, and all who live in it" (NIV). Upon seeing a shrine to an unknown God, Saint Paul reminded the Athenians that God didn't need that shrine. God's home was among us. "The God who made the world and everything in it," Acts 17:24 tells us, "[the one] who is Lord of heaven and earth, does not live in shrines made by human hands." And Jesus himself told followers to look only to the sparrow and the raven (along with those glorious wildflowers) for reminders of God at work.

Acts 17:14 says the created world bears *witness* to our Creator. And what do witnesses do? They call attention to. They testify. They point toward. That's how our animal friends—these saints of feather and fang and paw and hoof and scale and tail—can lead us to the thinnest of places.

———

Realizing our old dog had gone deaf wasn't as sad for me as perhaps it should have been. But having spent her life being terrorized by thunderstorms and our terrible, awful, no-good neighbors who think fireworks are appropriate in suburban streets, Sierra could now live without quaking through the summer months.

And her deafness meant something else. "The next voice she hears will be the voice of Jesus," I said chirpily. Trying to maintain that this was okay. That because of her fears of booming noises, going deaf was not a loss but a gain. That perhaps she wasn't as close to death as this might otherwise indicate. But as I said this, my eyes welled. Partly because it was true, but also because it pointed to how badly, how desperately *I* had wanted to hear the voice of Jesus, to find reassurance during a rather confusing time. I didn't want to *die* to hear it, but I wanted to know, somehow, that Jesus was with me and hearing my prayers about a big concern in my family.

I thought about this a few weeks later as I scrabbled along the gravel Prairie Path that runs through our town. Once the tracks for the train that took passengers from the south side of our suburb into Chicago, today the path welcomes walkers, strollers, bicyclists, joggers, dogs—and lots and lots of kids on their way to and from school. Coyotes use it. So do foxes, squirrels, rabbits, and raccoons. (And murderers. When I was a child, my friend found a dead body along the path. But that's another story.)

The best part about the path—to me—is that it weaves through short stretches of suburban life: over train tracks, along roads, by stores, through woods and reclaimed prairie, under expressways, and alongside homes. You can escape and imagine; a mind can wander and drift. But you are never far away from "real life."

That day as I walked, I listened to my favorite prayer app. During a prompt, I reminded Jesus how much I had longed to know he was indeed hearing my prayers, that he was Emmanuel—God *with* me. But as had been the case over the past several weeks of prayer, I got nothing. Nada.

That is, until a murder of crows began to caw-caw-caw furiously from the heights of the trees beside me. "Consider the ravens" (the crow's bigger, noisier corvid cousin), Jesus tells us in Luke 12:24.

And so I did.

Then, I remembered. Twenty years ago, West Nile virus struck and killed off most of the crows in our town. The ones who didn't die apparently escaped to less virus-y locales. Up until that point, they would gather in our front yard, fighting off robins who dared try to perch or nest in "their" trees. Not everyone was a fan of the crows—but I was. I loved their black sheen, their steely eyes, and even (perhaps especially) their ominous presence. Crows had added an edge to our neighborhood that was sorely missed. At least, by me. And so I asked God to bring them back. And the answer to that prayer had been nothing. Nada.

Except now, decades later, on a path in that same town, here they were. Crows, crows, and more crows. They came back. Perhaps God brought them back—per my request. Perhaps these new generations had long forgotten about their ancestors' struggle in these neighborhoods. Perhaps they were just stopping over. But as I watched and listened to these magnificent crows caw-cawing and chasing robins just as I remembered them, the space thinned.

All at once, I was twentysomething again, praying for the return of the crows. And I was my present age, praying for my family situation. And somehow, I was in the future, seeing the answer to my current prayer.

It was a weird, time-transcendent moment. But in it, I knew: Jesus heard me. God was with me. God was working. Even in the waiting.

———

Two years later, I stood on the porch with Sierra. I sobbed as I tugged her collar to lead her inside, to awaiting death. Her executioner—the kindly vet who came by to light candles, offer bon mots, and administer the shots that would ease Sierra of her suffering—waited in our living room with my family.

"You're about to hear the voice of Jesus," I told her. "Go to him when you do. He's there with Rocky and Blade, with Gus and Faith and Sven . . . Be nice when you meet them."

My words to Sierra in that moment may be mumbo jumbo to many people, some scrim of self-soothing at a time of sadness. I get it. Yet I believe our animals, even in their deaths, point to these other worlds. These worlds beyond or above—or very, very near. Where there will be no more suffering, no more sorrow, no more death.

And as my dog slipped from this world into the next—where I believe, for what it's worth, she waits in a liminal space—these worlds came very close. I could almost smell the redemption at hand.

11

REDEMPTION

CONSIDER THE DONKEYS

"Excuse me," the woman said. I turned from the llama toward the woman, squinting to see if I recognized her behind her mask. I didn't. Our outdoor live nativity services attracted lots of folks from the community—people who didn't regularly attend our church but, because of pandemic Christmas boredom, were drawn to the idea of a short walk-up Christmas service featuring animals (a llama even!).

"I'm Lisa," she said. "I liked what you said about Jesus saving the sheep and llamas too. Was nice to hear."

I laughed and admitted my nervousness about that line in my "Animal Eve" (as I was calling the services) message. "Not everyone appreciates talking about animals and salvation," I said as we went back to petting the sheep. "Not everyone understands what I mean."

Indeed, they don't. Jesus saves—and as I said in that message, Jesus was born to save not only *people* but every river, tree, cloud, planet, sheep, and llama. We tend to forget this, especially when we look at salvation and redemption as only about the soul and the afterlife and not about the here and now. That's when people get caught up in who has souls and who can "accept Jesus" and who gets to "go" to heaven.

Humans may be the ones made in the image of God. Humans may have the responsibility to care for the earth. Humans may be the ones commanded to share the love of Christ with friends and enemies alike. Humans may even be the only ones with souls (though animals clearly have something that enlivens and animates them, some essence of force or spirit). But humans are *not* the only ones Jesus came to "save," and humans are not the only part of the redemption plan that the Scriptures tell us God set in motion way back in the garden of Eden. *We* may talk as though this redemption is only for humans; however, the Scriptures do not.

Though the language of new creation passages may be figurative and symbolic, that *animals* are named points toward the inclusivity of God's redemption plan. Consider what Paul writes to the Romans about our "future glory":

> For the creation waits with eager longing for the revealing of the children of God; for the creation was subjected to futility, not of its own will but by the will of the one who subjected it, in hope that the creation itself will be set free from its bondage to decay and will obtain the freedom of the glory of the children of God. We know that the whole creation has been groaning in labor pains until now; and not only the creation, but we ourselves, who have the first fruits of the Spirit, groan inwardly while we wait for adoption, the redemption of our bodies. For in hope we were saved. (Romans 8:19–24)

We're *all* waiting, groaning, Paul writes, for redemption. We all hope for the day we are saved—fully. Every last bit of creation. We're all part of God's redemptive plan.

Surely this is why the prophets include animals so specifically in their visions of the restoration to come. Isaiah writes,

The wolf shall live with the lamb,
    the leopard shall lie down with the kid,
the calf and the lion and the fatling together,
    and a little child shall lead them.
The cow and the bear shall graze,
    their young shall lie down together;
    and the lion shall eat straw like the ox.
The nursing child shall play over the hole of
  the asp,
    and the weaned child shall put its hand
    on the adder's den.
They will not hurt or destroy
    on all my holy mountain;
for the earth will be full of the knowledge of
  the Lord
    as the waters cover the sea. (Isaiah 11:6–9)

The apostle John saw this image of the redeemed days and worlds to come: "Then I heard every creature in heaven and on earth and under the earth and in the sea, and all that is in them, singing, 'To the one seated on the throne and to the Lamb be blessing and honor and glory and might forever and ever!'" (Revelation 5:13).

But of course, God's redemption plan isn't only about the far-off future or "end times." God's redemption plan includes the eventual end to pain and suffering, but it also includes a way to turn the pain and suffering into something *good.*

And this plan—to not let evil get the last say—began the moment Adam and Eve bit the fruit from the tree. God's redemption plan worked through the covenants. God's plan worked through the law and the prophets, and in the birth, life, ministry, death, and resurrection of Jesus Christ. All throughout the Scriptures, the redemption plan was meant to work through God's people. Their actions, their love, their obedience, their trust were all meant to turn a wrong world right.

The same is meant for us today. Jesus's call to love God and our neighbors, to turn the other cheek, and to love our enemies; Jesus's modeling of healing, of inclusion, of feeding the hungry, and of letting the outcasts learn at his feet and sit at his table. All these were about redemption, about taking what had gone very, very wrong and making it better—good, if not yet very good.

And animals have a lot to teach about what that looks like.

———

Redemption is a big word. It can mean many things, including making something better, more worthy or acceptable. It can mean—as I used earlier—saved from evil. It can mean an exchange of money for goods. But my favorite definition of *redemption* comes from the very end of the book of Genesis.

After the brothers who sold Joseph into slavery beg for his forgiveness, Joseph offers these words of deep mercy and grace to his once treacherous and now incredulous brothers: "Even though you intended to do harm to me, God intended it for good" (Genesis 50:20).

Now this story—like so many Bible stories and passages—raises all kinds of questions about sovereignty and causality, the origins of evil and the general ways of God. While we could debate that all day long, what I hope we can agree to see is a long-mistreated man who is able to look back on terrible suffering and see redemption. Joseph is testifying to God's ability to turn an act of cruelty, of evil, of destruction into something for the kindness, goodness, and betterment of the world.

And *that* is the redemption I'm talking about. In the story of Joseph and his brothers, we see the same redemption we see in the story of the trafficked Queen Esther (read it if you haven't!). We see redemption in the story of Daniel and in story after story after story with Jesus.

As it turns out, it's also the redemption we see in the story of pit bulls.

———

When sportswriter Jim Goran wrote *The Lost Dogs*, his marvelous book about the new lives of the dogs saved from football player Michael Vick's heinous dogfighting compound, he included *redemption* in the subtitle, which is as spot-on as one can get. And Bronwen Dickey—incidentally, the daughter of poet James Dickey, who wrote so beautifully about animals in heaven—spent much time detailing the redemption of the American pit bull terrier in her marvelous book, *Pit Bull*.

Many animals have made major comebacks. Species have looked extinction in the eye and fought back or have seen their reputations restored. But few other animals have taught more about redemption—in every meaning of the world—than pit bulls.

Though in the early twentieth century, pit bulls were seen as wonderful family dogs and even Hollywood stars, according to Dickey, we can blame racism for the change in the (white) public's perception of them. While pit bulls were once hugely popular, when Black families noticed how wonderful the dogs were, a kind of dog-world "white flight" happened. Pits became viewed—by white people—as dangerous and as ticking time bombs. This myth was based largely on racist ideas and assumptions that these dogs were all now being used to fight or for protection. Surely these dogs were monsters!

This attitude simmered for decades, but it came to a head in the 1990s and early 2000s. But then a couple things happened: Hurricane Katrina decimated New Orleans and NFL "star" Michael Vick got arrested.

When humane societies headed to New Orleans to rescue stranded dogs, they were met with a plethora of pit bulls, lost or left behind by desperate owners in the mostly Black communities that took the biggest hits from levee failures. (Jesmyn Ward tells the story of a family of one such pit bull in her dazzling book, *Salvage the Bones*—although unlike many of the dogs rescued in New Orleans, the pit bull in *Salvage the Bones* was beloved but used to fight.) While at first some white rescuers were nervous about the pit bulls, according to Dickey, they discovered these dogs were amazing. Friendly. Silly. Snuggly. Smart. The rescuers brought back not only the dogs but the *stories* about how terrific pit bulls were. And the narrative began to change.

When Vick's dogs were led out of his dogfighting compound, something else happened. The public—having already heard stories about the torture these dogs endured—did not see fighting monsters. They saw adorable, sweet, and scared dogs emerge and jump into animal control vans.

Though some of those abused animals didn't make it out alive—or even to adoptive homes—forty-seven of the fifty-one pit bulls taken from Vick's dogfighting operation were saved. And not only were they saved; while some stayed in sanctuaries, many went to families. All forty-seven went on to have lives full of love and safety and to become mighty "breed ambassadors"—and stories of lost dogs found and redeemed.

These Katrina and "Vick" dogs turned the tide for pit bulls everywhere. To paraphrase Joseph, what the destructive powers of a hurricane, the societal failures that forced so many good people to leave their good dogs behind in tragedy, and the evil actions of an abusive dogfighting leader meant for evil, God used for good (Genesis 50:20).

I don't want to minimize the horror of Katrina or of Vick's actions. This broken world is full of corrupt people who try their best to let evil do its worst, but God doesn't stand for that. God is in the phoenix-from-ashes business. This is what redemption looks like. We see that throughout the Scriptures and in the resurrection of Jesus, and we see it in the story of pit bulls, even if imperfectly.

My town teems with rescued pit bulls. I count five on my small square block. At one point there were six. There are only two golden retrievers. One black lab. One Rottweiler. That's *amazing*. Though pit bulls are still disproportionately "put down" in shelters and though certainly they still face discrimination (especially when owned by Black or Hispanic families), the tide has turned. Where once pits were canine enemy number one, pit bulls now sell products. They're on dog food bags. They're movie stars. That's redemption.

I hate that racism played such a huge role in the demise of pit bulls. And I hate that because of racism, it was only when white rescue workers noted how good these dogs were that other white people believed them. Black families have been singing pit bulls' praises for a long time!

Yet whenever lies get righted, we find redemption. Whenever lives get saved, we find redemption. Whenever images are restored, we find redemption. Whenever one group or person finds a reason to repent, we start on the road toward redemption.

In the current world, we still have a long way to go. No redemption here is perfect. That's why we still long so desperately for the life beyond and the world to come. And yet in the work of redemption, in the stories of Joseph and of pit bulls, we see signs of that future world, of what I believe is the very kingdom of God. Redemption doesn't excuse the evil that precedes it. Redemption doesn't celebrate it. Redemption doesn't make the injustice or evil "worth it." But somehow, the miracle and mystery of redemption allow us to see the good—the very hand of God at work—in it all. And they help us understand that our animal friends were always included in God's redemption plan for this world.

———

With a picture of her fuzzy-faced, gray "next-door donkey," popular Bible teacher Beth Moore tweeted, "Indeed I spoke the priestly blessing over her this morning. The Lord's face is bright enough to shine on donkeys, too."

Amen and amen. I was tempted to paraphrase Jesus and type "Consider the donkeys . . ." in the comment section. But there were already about a billion comments, so instead of typing, I decided to just, well, consider the donkeys.

Indeed, there is something so lovely about the words of Numbers 6:24–26 falling on a donkey's ears: "The Lord bless you and keep you; the Lord make his face to shine upon you, and be gracious to you; the Lord lift up his countenance upon you, and give you peace."

Moore is right. Animals are and have always been included in God's blessings—and in God's redemption plan. This is good news not only for us animal lovers but for everyone and every creature.

Animals know the suffering of this world just as we do. They experience abuse, they lose habitats, they know fear, and they feel pain. But they also know their savior, their redeemer. The Scriptures show us this—and we can see it on the face of every trusting rescued pit bull and on that blessed donkey.

Indeed, we see it in the story of all creatures, of all creation. God at work. God redeeming. All of it. All of us. All the time.

Appendix

FURTHER THOUGHTS ON ANIMALS IN THE BIBLE

I fell for it. The group assignment in our theology class was to play Bible translator. Our task, based on the real-life experience of our professor's parents, was to decide how we would translate the phrase "lion and the lamb" to a culture that had never seen a lion or a lamb. Would it be best to stick with the literal lion and lamb? Or perhaps change it up to python and pig—two animals with which folks in this culture were intimately familiar? Or perhaps it was best to make it general and translate it as "predator and prey"?

My vote was for "python and pig" (what an amazing image!). I lost. As did those who stuck with "lion and lamb" or chose "predator and prey." Turns out, while we got caught up in literalism and linguistics, we missed the point—though some would call it a trick.

We failed to ask, "Is 'lion and the lamb' a phrase that's actually even in the Bible? Like, do the two words appear together?"

The answer, my friends, is no.

Although I'm *pretty* sure I had a picture of a lion, a lamb, and a child playing together on my nursery wall and I know I've sung about and referenced the lion and the lamb all the time, it's not a phrase used anywhere in the Bible. Isaiah gives us pictures of *wolves* and lambs together and a *calf* and a lion being led by a child (Isaiah 11:6). And Revelation 5 connects the lion of Judah and the sacrificial lamb into one image of Jesus. And of course, lions and lambs appear on altars and in dens and all sorts of places in Scripture—but never together. Never how we imagine. This Christian catchphrase is nothing more than a mixed metaphor.

My classmates and I realized this seminary sleight-of-hand trick with a groan, and one of my creative classmates penned an amazing "Python of Judah" tune (which both cracks me up and moves me, as I'm sure the python of Judah could cure my fear of snakes once and for all). Yet this experience sparked something else in me. It made me realize just how often we get the Bible wrong—about all things, of course, but particularly about animals.

Somehow, most of us are led to believe that animals in the Bible are *secondary*. We think their role is mere symbolism or that their presence is utility or illustration. And yet that view is skewed—dangerously so, I believe—by a belief that God's purpose in creating and then rescuing and redeeming this world is all about us: *humanity*. Yet God's purpose, in fact, is about all of us: *all of us, all of it, all creation*. Animals. Plants. Rocks. Trees. Coral reefs. Mountain ranges. Planets. Stars. Moons. Black holes. All of it.

═══════

As has been my practice for the past several years, in 2020, I read through the Bible. I don't do this because I'm so devout or legalistic. I do it because if I didn't follow a regimented, detailed plan that kept me reading five days a week, fifty-two weeks a year, I might not read the Bible at all. Well, not in any kind of consistent fashion. I lack the discipline to get up every morning and *read* the Scriptures on my own. So in the same way my ridiculous Apple Watch shames me into moving more than I want to or reminds me I haven't taken my daily walk, my little weekly tracking sheet keeps me on goal.

And the goal, for what it's worth, is to read. That's it. Not to expect something big or transformative will happen. Not to expect that every day I'll read something new or surprising. Not even to feel particularly inspired or close to God. Though I am a prodigious underliner and margin-scribbler, I don't journal or pray as I go. The discipline is just to read. And so I do. Year after year.

The year 2020 was different, of course, so noted by the small word *coronavirus* scribbled at week ten on my paper plan. Week ten was not when I first heard or worried about COVID. Week ten was when my bit of the world shut down. When my kids came home from school. When my church stopped meeting in person. Two weeks later, week twelve, my state (Illinois) went into total lockdown. We worried about toilet paper. We began wearing masks. We figured this was all just necessary for a couple of weeks until the "curve" bent and the virus went away. Nearly a year later, that all felt like foolishness.

Even though I believed it would be short-lived, I added the note at week ten because it felt significant. I've lived through lots of *epi*demics, but this was my first *pan*demic. I figured I'd want to know what it was like to read the Scriptures during a pandemic that kept us locked down. I reminded myself to add another mark when this ended—you know, in *a few weeks*.

Months later, as I checked off the boxes for the fifty-second week of 2020 with no other mark in sight, I realized: yes, you read the Bible differently during a global pandemic. At least, you do when your life has been otherwise full of relative comfort and definite privilege. When daily death numbers stagger the imagination, when life as we know it comes to an abrupt halt (and you realize you can't, won't, and shouldn't ever go back to "normal"), and when important social issues such as Black Lives Matter come to a head in the midst of it, you notice things. You appreciate things that the Bible has to say about mass human suffering and injustice.

In the same way, when you begin forming an idea for a project about animals and God four months into that wild year, you *also* read the Bible differently. While I always knew the Bible had lots to say about animals, I never really noticed the absolute significance and centrality of their role in the Scriptures—particularly given that the Bible is set in cultures that didn't anthropomorphize animals the way we do.

And so during 2020, when I read through the Bible, I underlined and noted and added plenty of *!!!* in the margins about illness, selfishness, injustice, mercy—and animals. Let me tell you: there's a lot on all of these topics.

Simply put, there's a shocking number of passages about animals in Scripture. We know the big stories. We know the naming of the animals in the creation story—and the horrible *killing* of the animals in the flood story. Animals become sign, seal, and symbol of covenant. Animals testify to God's might (and weirdness) and save prophets like Jonah and Daniel. Balaam's ass saves his ass. Animals portray God's power during the exodus and God's provision in the wilderness. Animals bear witness (and add comfort, I like to imagine) to the birth of Christ, and an animal bears the burden of Christ in his triumphal entry. Animals carry demons off a cliff—and invite a Syrophoenician woman to banter with Jesus.

I could go on and on. Animals are *everywhere* in the Bible, and their presence means more than we think.

In a talk for authors and publishing industry executives, Eugene Peterson shared language's power to personalize and relationalize God, lest we fall into abstract "godtalk." As I read through the Scriptures with an eye toward the animals, it occurred to me: this is what the animal images do for us. They personalize—perhaps even *animalize*—God so that we understand what we otherwise cannot. Although animals do not bear the image of God, God uses animals to convey *God's* image, to communicate God's qualities, and to reveal God's nature. It's curious, and a bit shocking. Then again, God uses fire, water, burning bushes, wind, bread, rocks, princes, and paupers to show Godself. Considering that, an eagle isn't so strange.

Thus, in the Scriptures we see God the Father as eagle and lion. We see Jesus as lion, lamb, and mother hen. And of course, we see the Spirit as dove.

In offering animal images of God, God graciously gives us what Peterson suggests—a complex and perhaps confusing but also a relational, relatable image of God that both makes sense in our world and also takes us *out* of this world.

When God reminded Moses that God carried the people out and *up* on eagle's wings "and brought [them] to [Godself]" (Exodus 19:4), God invited Moses to look higher than the mountain he stood on—up into the sky, the realm of mighty birds of prey—and *imagine* the power and the might of a God who does beyond what we can think of or envision actually happening in this world. In Ephesians 3:20, Saint Paul calls us to do the same more than a millennium later. When Jesus mourns Jerusalem and connects himself to a mother hen, Jesus offers a picture of a God not stuck on gender or embarrassed by roles. And when the fiery, roaring, rushing Holy Ghost makes manifest in a dove—the cheapest of temple offerings—we see, as we do in Jesus, a God who relates to the lowliest, the humblest. We see a God who also sees power in humility.

Time and again, we see that God uses animals not only to do great things in Scripture but to reveal God's greatness and goodness. This is why, although that seminary classroom assignment was a trick, the idea of properly translating animal names *does* matter. How we understand the words and the images is how we understand God.

=====

It can't be coincidence that the Scriptures begin and end with animals. We first meet them just twenty verses into Genesis 1—after God created a world that would sustain the creatures of the sky, sea, and land. And the Scriptures leave us with animals representing both goodness and evil. (I should pause here to talk about one of my *least* favorite passages in Scripture, in which Jesus calls sexual abusers, liars, witchcraft practitioners, murderers, and idolators "dogs." But Jesus was just speaking to his time. *Dogs* was an insult then. Moving on.) And they appear this way throughout.

Animals are not always (often) treated well in the Scriptures. Neither are people. We see animals dying en masse—often seemingly at the hand of God. We see animals suffering under a broken world but also benefiting from God's grace and redemption. That they are often brutal signs of the covenant is hard to read, but this makes animals *part* of the covenant. Perhaps not as people are—but participants nevertheless.

After all, on the fifth and sixth "days" of creation, God called the animals not just good but *very* good. And even after the fall, God used these very good creatures to speak to who God is, and God accepted their praise as worship. And God uses the animals—again and again—as exhibits A, B, and C of God's fierce protection and tender care over this world.

When God *finally* speaks to Job, battered and beleaguered but faithful to the end, God takes Job through all of creation (as Job knows it) and offers some of the most gorgeous writing about animals ever, which makes this long passage a great place to end a book:

> *Do you hunt the prey for the lioness*
> *   and satisfy the hunger of the lions*
> *when they crouch in their dens*
> *   or lie in wait in a thicket?*
> *Who provides food for the raven*
> *   when its young cry out to God*
> *   and wander about for lack of food?*

Do you know when the mountain goats give
  birth?
    Do you watch when the doe bears her
      fawn?
Do you count the months till they bear?
    Do you know the time they give birth?
They crouch down and bring forth their young;
    their labor pains are ended.
Their young thrive and grow strong in the
  wilds;
    they leave and do not return.
Who let the wild donkey go free?
    Who untied its ropes?
I gave it the wasteland as its home,
    the salt flats as its habitat.
It laughs at the commotion in the town;
    it does not hear a driver's shout.
It ranges the hills for its pasture
    and searches for any green thing.
Will the wild ox consent to serve you?
    Will it stay by your manger at night?
Can you hold it to the furrow with a harness?
    Will it till the valleys behind you?
Will you rely on it for its great strength?
    Will you leave your heavy work to it?
Can you trust it to haul in your grain
    and bring it to your threshing floor?

The wings of the ostrich flap joyfully,
    though they cannot compare
    with the wings and feathers of the stork.
She lays her eggs on the ground
    and lets them warm in the sand,
unmindful that a foot may crush them,
    that some wild animal may trample them.
She treats her young harshly, as if they were
    not hers;
        she cares not that her labor was in vain,
for God did not endow her with wisdom
    or give her a share of good sense.
Yet when she spreads her feathers to run,
    she laughs at horse and rider.
Do you give the horse its strength
    or clothe its neck with a flowing mane?
Do you make it leap like a locust,
    striking terror with its proud snorting?
It paws fiercely, rejoicing in its strength,
    and charges into the fray.
It laughs at fear, afraid of nothing;
    it does not shy away from the sword.
The quiver rattles against its side,
    along with the flashing spear and lance.
In frenzied excitement it eats up the ground;
    it cannot stand still when the trumpet
        sounds.

At the blast of the trumpet it snorts, "Aha!"
  It catches the scent of battle from afar,
  the shout of commanders and the battle
    cry.
Does the hawk take flight by your wisdom
  and spread its wings toward the south?
Does the eagle soar at your command
  and build its nest on high?
It dwells on a cliff and stays there at night;
  a rocky crag is its stronghold.
From there it looks for food;
  its eyes detect it from afar.
Its young ones feast on blood,
  and where the slain are, there it is.

In this passage, God invites Job to learn something about God by looking to the animals. I believe this invitation extends to us, whether we're looking to the animals in our world or the animals in Scripture. When we read the Bible—the great love and rescue story of God's people and God's world—we can read it with an eye toward the sparrow, the donkey, the lamb, and the lion. Their creatureliness might captivate us, and their saintliness might shine through. Through them, we might begin to see the God who created them in a whole new light.

Acknowledgments

Though this book pays homage to the saints of feather and fang (and snout and claw and fur and hackle), my life includes plenty of saints of skin and well-tended smiles. I'm so grateful for the many good saints (and sinners!) God threw my way. Thanks to:

My amazing colleagues at Elmhurst Christian Reformed Church. Working with hilarious, creative, smart, quarrelsome, caring, and prayer-centered people makes coming to work every day pure joy.

My Northern Seminary cohort. If these folks are the future of the church, she's in good (and super fun) hands. Thanks especially for the group chat. Who knew you could laugh so hard in seminary? Anyway, let's book a party bus and plan a reunion.

My agent, Adria Goetz. Her clients call her a fairy godmother for good reason! Adria makes magic happen and is so supportive and encouraging and wise and discerning.

My editor, Valerie Weaver-Zercher, and everyone at Broadleaf Books. Thanks for offering the opportunity to write this book and for your magnificent guidance on it.

My writer friends at Ink Creative Collective and in all those Facebook groups! What a wonderful thing it is to have a community of writers to make us feel less alone (and less weird).

Cathy McNeil Stein, for your early read and comments.

The fine folks at Peace for Pits. During the process of writing this book, my family grieved the death of one dog (RIP, Sierra!) and rejoiced in the adoption of two new dogs, who came to us via Peace for Pits. I was reminded again how animal rescuers do the Lord's work.

My parents, for raising me to love animals.

My husband, Rafi, for loving animals as much as I do.

My kids—Henrik, Greta, and Fredrik—for being the very best creatures of all time. Being your mom has revealed more to me about God and love and joy and grace and mercy and redemption and all these things than even the animals can. But I promise I won't write a book about that. I love you.

Notes

Chapter 1

12 **"every now and then"**: Jeffery Kluger, "Why Dogs and Humans Love Each Other More Than Anyone Else," *Time*, July 20, 2018, https://time.com/5342964/human-bond-dog-thoughts/.

12 **"If you didn't need"**: Kluger.

13 **"And it's not just because"**: Theresa Fisher, "Brain Scans Reveal What Dogs Really Think of Us," *Mic*, February 13, 2020, https://www.mic.com/articles/104474/brain-scans-reveal-what-dogs-really-think-of-us.

13 **"dogs were more inclined"**: Berit Brogaard, "Can Animals Love?," *Psychology Today*, February 24, 2014, https://www.psychologytoday.com/us/blog/the-mysteries-love/201402/can-animals-love.

14 **"increased activity in regions"**: Brogaard.

17 **"Some 70 percent of humans"**: "Is the Momma Bear Really the Most Protective Animal Mother?," Motherhood: In Point of Fact (website), accessed April 16, 2020, http://motherhoodinpointoffact.com/momma-bear-protective-animal-mother/.

Chapter 2

28 **"Sheep are actually surprisingly intelligent"**: Harriet Constable, "Sheep Are Not Stupid and They Are Not Helpless Either," BBC, accessed October 22, 2020, http://www.bbc.com/earth/story/20170418-sheep-are-not-stupid-and-they-are-not-helpless-either.

Chapter 3

39 **"habitual and firm disposition"**: *Catechism of the Catholic Church*, accessed October 30, 2020, https://www.catholicculture.org/culture/library/catechism/index.cfm?recnum=5026.

Chapter 4

51 **"I am drawn to such dramas"**: Maxine Kumin, "Nurture," Poetry Foundation (website), accessed November 2, 2020, https://www.poetryfoundation.org/poetrymagazine/poems/36908/nurture.

52 **"Montgomery writes in her book *How to Be a Good Creature"***: Montgomery, Sy, *How to Be a Good Creature: A Memoir in Thirteen Animals.* (New York: Houghton Mifflin Harcort, 2018), 24.

54 **"When something surprises you"**: "The Immeasurable Experience of Delight," *Setmore* (blog), accessed November 15, 2020, https://www.setmore.com/blog/.

56 **"an eccentric delight"**: Phoebe Weston, "Prickly Business: The Hedgehog Highway That Knits a Village Together," *Guardian*, accessed October 15, 2020, https://tinyurl.com/ytudhzba.

57 **"They are saving the lives"**: Weston.

58 **"Isabel Houselander"**: Weston.

Chapter 5

62 **"Today, wildlife experts believe"**: Evan Garcia, "Why Are Coyotes Thriving in the Chicago Area?," WTTW, December 27, 2017, https://news.wttw.com /2017/12/27/why-are-coyotes-thriving-chicago-area.

66 **"While certainly God"**: "Animal Adaptations: Teachers Guide," University of Southern Indiana, accessed October 17, 2020, https://www.usi.edu/ media/1751789/AnimalAdap.pdf.

67 **"This is not to say"**: Note: I have zero interest in diving too deeply into the realm of original sin or "the fall." But I do believe God created a very good world—and I also believe the world became corrupted by evil. Discussing the particulars would fill more pages than I've got!

67 **"Perhaps it was only after death"**: Of course, believers of God's omniscience could also argue God created animals this way *knowing* we would "fall."

70 **"According to a report"**: "Humanity Has Wiped Out 60% of Animal Populations since 1970, Report Finds," *Guardian*, accessed December 6, 2020, https://tinyurl.com/3hpe74af.

Chapter 6

75 **"Giant forces that had been building up"**: National Geographic Staff, "The Deadliest Tsunami in History?,"

National Geographic.com, accessed December 7, 2020, https://www.nationalgeographic.com/news/2004/12/deadliest-tsunami-in-history/.

76 **"Even though the waters"**: "Did Animals Sense the Tsunami?," *Al Jazeera*, accessed December 7, 2020, https://www.aljazeera.com/news/2005/1/2/did-animals-sense-the-tsunami.

76 **"Animals can sense disaster"**: "Did Animals Sense the Tsunami?"

84 **"satisfy two basic functions"**: Brandon Ambrosio, "Do Humans Have a Religion Instinct?," BBC, May 29, 2019, https://www.bbc.com/future/article/20190529-do-humans-have-a-religion-instinct.

85 **"Say you're out in the savannah"**: Ambrosio.

86 **"endorphin-triggering activation"**: Ambrosio.

88 **"We can shrug off"**: I have a hard time talking about dog breeders. I appreciate breed distinctions and can applaud the breeders committed to conserving the standards and intentions of their breeds. But there are so many irresponsible dog "breeders" who do it to make money that it has nearly ruined the whole gamut for me. Adopt, don't shop.

88 **"The world is *charged*"**: Gerard Manley Hopkins, "God's Grandeur," Poetry Foundation (website), accessed November 17, 2020, https://www.poetryfoundation.org/poems/44395/gods-grandeur.

Chapter 7

94 **"Bats and snakes both appear"**: "Top 10 Animals That Scare Us the Most," Animal Planet, accessed

172

December 2, 2020, http://www.animalplanet.com/
wild-animals/2-rattlesnake/.

94 **"snakes are nothing"**: Justin Breen, "Chicago Is
Slithering with Snakes, but Don't Be Afraid, Expert
Says," DNAInfo, April 5, 2015, https://tinyurl.com/
2y2zkwtx.

96 **"According to one Australian"**: Sharon Kennedy
and Arthur Muhl, "Snakes Give Definite Signs
about Their Mood, Says Expert," ABC News Australia, September 21, 2016, https://tinyurl.com/
vvwa97fw.

Chapter 8

108 **"The first time I scrolled"**: Neal Agarwal, The Deep
Sea (website), accessed December 26, 2020, https://
neal.fun/deep-sea/.

109 **"Life can survive"**: Agarwal.

109 **"developer with a passion"**: Neal Agarwal, "Hi
I'm Neal," accessed December 26, 2020, https://
nealagarwal.me.

112 **"not that huge"**: Jacob Wallenberg, *Min son på
galejan* [My son on the galley], 1781, quoted in
"Kraken: The Legendary Sea Monster," Psy Minds,
October 24, 2019, https://psy-minds.com/kraken
-the-legendary-sea-monster/.

115 **"The Smithsonian shows me"**: "Biodiversity in the
Baltic Sea," Smithsonian Ocean Portal, accessed
December 26, 2020, https://ocean.si.edu/ocean-life/
fish/biodiversity-baltic-sea.

Chapter 9

128   **"Fairy tales are more than true"**: Neil Gaiman, *Coraline* (New York: HarperAlley, 2009), epigraph.

128   **"First somewhat substantial snow"**: Kristin Du Mez (@kkdumez), Twitter, December 30, 2020, https://twitter.com/kkdumez/status/1344324729952468993.

Chapter 10

135   **"are locales where the distance"**: Eric Wiener, "When Heaven and Earth Come Closer," *New York Times*, March 11, 2012, https://tinyurl.com/yem7cvzu.

137   **"Certainly not the way the Egyptians did"**: "Cats Rule in Ancient Egypt," *National Geographic Kids*, accessed January 8, 2021, https://kids.national geographic.com/explore/cats-rule-in-ancient-egypt/.

Chapter 11

153   **"next-door donkey"**: Beth Moore (@BethMooreLPM), Twitter, October 6, 2020, https://twitter.com/Beth MooreLPM/status/1313461101183590400.

Appendix

160   **"godtalk"**: Eugene Peterson, "What Are Writers Good For?" (lecture), Alive Communications Authors and Industry Executives, July 9, 2006.

163   **"Do you hunt the prey for the lioness"**: Job 38:39–39:30 NIV.